PYTHON PROGRAMMING

Beginners Guide

SUNDARRAJAN M, MANI DEEPAK CHOUDHRY,
JEEVANANDHAM S, AKSHYA JOTHI

ISBN 979-8-89363-696-3

CONTENTS

CHAPTER 1

ALGORITHMIC PROBLEM SOLVING

Algorithms, Structural elements (statements, state, control flow, functions), notation (pseudo code, flow chart, programming language), algorithmic problem solving, modest strategies for developing algorithms (iteration, recursion). Explanatory problems: find minimum in a list, insert a card in a list of sorted cards, Guess an integer number in a range, Towers of Hanoi.

1. PROBLEM SOLVING

The process of assessing the situation, evaluating the source of the problem, finding, prioritizing, and choosing possible solutions for a remedy, and incorporating a solution is referred to as problem solving. The methodical approach to defining the problem and producing a variety of solutions is known as problem solving. The problem-solving process begins with problem requirements and concludes with a working application.

When it comes to solving problems, it's often necessary to consider pragmatics, or how context influences meaning, as well as semantics, or how the problem is interpreted. The ability to comprehend the problem's end objective and the laws that could be used to solve it is crucial to its resolution. Often a dilemma necessitates abstract thought or the creation of a novel solution.

1.1 PROBLEM SOLVING TECHNIQUES

Problem solving technique is a set of techniques that helps in providing logic for solving a problem. Problem-solving techniques are the actions taken to identify the obstacles that stand in the way of achieving one's own objectives.

Problem Solving Techniques

Problem solving can be expressed in the form of

- Algorithms.
- Flowcharts.
- Pseudo codes.
- Programs

1.2 ALGORITHM

A complete range of well-defined, computer-implementable guidelines used to resolve a series of problems or execute a procedure is known as an algorithm. Algorithms are often clear and are used to specify how equations, data processing, automatic reasoning, and other tasks should be done. It is defined as a sequence of instructions that describe a method for solving a problem. In other words, it is a step-by-step procedure for solving a problem.

Properties of Algorithms

- Should be written in simple English
- Each and every instruction should be precise and unambiguous.
- Instructions in an algorithm should not be repeated infinitely.
- Algorithm should conclude after a finite number of steps.
- Should have an end point
- Derived results should be obtained only after the algorithm terminates.

Qualities of a good algorithm

The following are the primary factors that are often used to judge the quality of the algorithms:

- Time – To execute a program, the computer system takes some amount of time. The lesser is the time required, the better is the algorithm.
- Memory – To execute a program, computer system takes some amount of memory space. The lesser is the memory required, the better is the algorithm.
- Accuracy – Multiple algorithms may provide suitable or correct solutions to a given problem, some of these may provide more accurate results than others, and such algorithms may be suitable.

Example:

Write an algorithm to print "Good Morning"

Step 1: Start

Step 2: Display "Good Morning"

Step 3: Stop

1.3. BUILDING BLOCKS OF ALGORITHMS (statements, state, control flow, functions)

Algorithms can be constructed from basic building blocks namely, sequence, selection and iteration.

1.3.1 Statements

Statement is a single action in a computer. In a computer statements might include some of the following actions:

- Input data-information given to the program
- Process data-perform operation on a given input
- Output data-processed result

1.3.2 State

Transition from one process to another process under specified condition with in a time is called state.

1.3.3 Control flow

The process of executing the individual statements in a given order is called control flow. The control can be executed in three ways

- Sequence
- Selection
- Iteration

Sequence

All the instructions are executed one after another is called sequence execution.

Example:

Add two numbers:

Step 1: Start

Step 2: get a,b

Step 3: calculate c=a+b

Step 4: Display c

Step 5: Stop

Selection

A selection statement causes the program control to be transferred to a specific part of the program based upon the condition.

If the conditional test is true, one part of the program will be executed, otherwise it will execute the other part of the program.

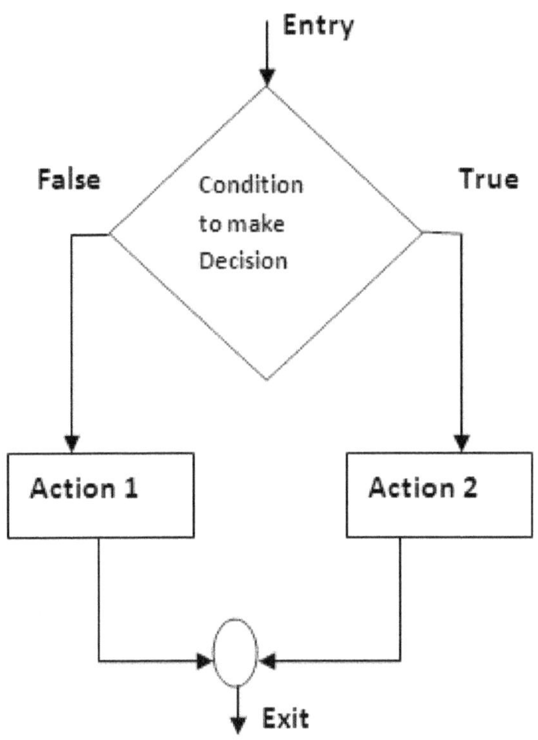

Example

Write an algorithm to check whether he is eligible to vote?

Step 1: Start

Step 2: Get age

Step 3: if age >= 18 print "Eligible to vote"

Step 4: else print "Not eligible to vote"

Step 5: Stop

Iteration

In some programs, certain set of statements are executed again and again based upon conditional test. i.e, executed more than one time. This type of execution is called looping or iteration.

Example

Write an algorithm to print all-natural numbers up to n

Step 1: Start

Step 2: get n value.

Step 3: initialize i=1

Step 4: if (i<=n) go to step 5 else go to step 7

Step 5: Print i value and increment i value by 1

Step 6: go to step 4

Step 7: Stop

1.3.4 Functions

Function is a sub program which consists of block of code (set of instructions) that performs a particular task.

For complex problems, the problem is been divided into smaller and simpler tasks during algorithm design.

Benefits of Using Functions

- Reduction in line of code
- Code reuse
- Better readability
- Information hiding
- Easy to debug and test
- Improved maintainability

Example:

Algorithm for addition of two numbers using function

Main function()

Step 1: Start

Step 2: Call the function add()

Step 3: Stop

sub function add()

Step 1: Function start

Step 2: Get a, b Values

Step 3: add c=a+b

Step 4: Print c

Step 5: Return

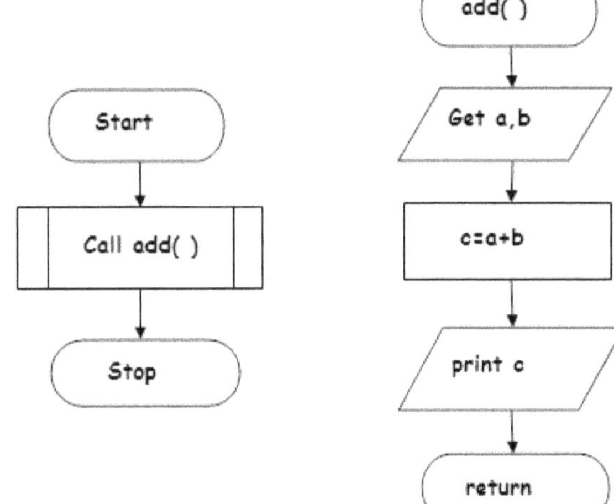

1.4. NOTATIONS

1.4.1 Flowchart

Flow chart is defined as graphical representation of the logic for problem solving.

The purpose of flowchart is making the logic of the program clear in a visual representation.

Symbol	Symbol Name	Description
	Flow Lines	Used to connect symbols
	Terminal	Used to start, pause or halt in the program logic
	Input/output	Represents the information entering or leaving the system
	Processing	Represents arithmetic and logical instructions
	Decision	Represents a decision to be made
	Connector	Used to Join different flow lines
	Sub function	used to call function

Rules for drawing a flowchart

- The flowchart should be clear, neat and easy to follow.
- The flowchart must have a logical start and finish.\Only one flow line should come out from a process symbol.

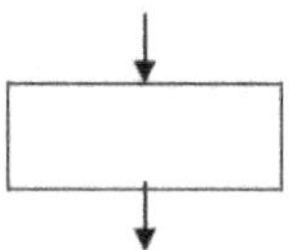

- Only one flow line should enter a decision symbol. However, two or three flow lines may leave the decision symbol.

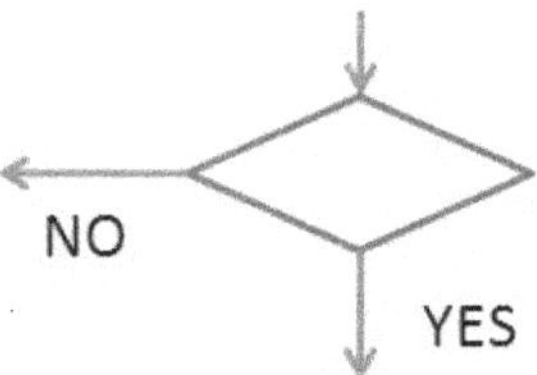

- Only one flow line is used with a terminal symbol.

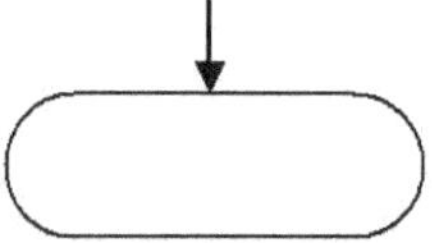

- Within standard symbols, write briefly and precisely.
- Intersection of flow lines should be avoided.

Advantages of flowchart:

1. **Communication:-** Flowcharts are better way of communicating the logic of a system to all concerned.
2. **Effective analysis:-** With the help of flowchart, problem can be analyzed in more effective way.
3. **Proper documentation:-** Program flowcharts serve as a good program documentation, which is needed for various purposes.

4. **Efficient Coding:-** The flowcharts act as a guide or blueprint during the systems analysis and program development phase.
5. **Proper Debugging:-** The flowchart helps in debugging process.
6. **Efficient Program Maintenance:-** The maintenance of operating program becomes easy with the help of flowchart. It helps the programmer to put efforts more efficiently on that part.

Disadvantages of flow chart:

1. **Complex logic:-** Sometimes, the program logic is quite complicated. In that case, flowchart becomes complex and clumsy.
2. **Alterations and Modifications:-** If alterations are required the flowchart may require re-drawing completely.
3. **Reproduction:-** As the flowchart symbols cannot be typed, reproduction of flowchart becomes a problem.
4. **Cost:-** For large application the time and cost of flowchart drawing becomes costly.

1.4.2 Pseudocode

- Pseudo code consists of short, readable and formally styled English languages used for explain an algorithm.
- It does not include details like variable declaration, subroutines.
- It is easier to understand for the programmer or non-programmer to understand the general working of the program, because it is not based on any programming language.
- It gives us the sketch of the program before actual coding.
- It is not a machine readable
- Pseudo code can't be compiled and executed.
- There is no standard syntax for pseudo code.

Guidelines for writing pseudo code

- Write one statement per line
- Capitalize initial keyword
- Indent to hierarchy
- End multiline structure
- Keep statements language independent

Common keywords used in pseudocode

The following gives common keywords used in pseudocodes.

- **//:** This keyword used to represent a comment.
- **BEGIN, END:** Begin is the first statement and end are the last statement.
- **INPUT, GET, READ:** The keyword is used to inputting data.
- **COMPUTE, CALCULATE:** used for calculation of the result of the given expression.
- **ADD, SUBTRACT, INITIALIZE:** used for addition, subtraction and initialization.
- **OUTPUT, PRINT, DISPLAY:** It is used to display the output of the program.
- **IF, ELSE, ENDIF:** used to make decision.
- **WHILE, ENDWHILE:** used for iterative statements.
- **FOR, ENDFOR:** Another iterative incremented/decremented tested automatically.

Syntax for if else:	Example: Greates of two numbers
IF (condition)THEN	BEGIN READ a,b
statement	IF (a>b) THEN
...	DISPLAY a is greater
ELSE	ELSE
statement	DISPLAY b is greater
...	END IF
ENDIF	END

Syntax for For:	Example: Print n natural numbers

FOR(*start-value to end-value*) DO
 	
   statement
 	
   ...
 	
ENDFOR
	BEGIN GET n
	
	INITIALIZE i=1
	
	FOR (i<=n) DO
	
	   PRINT i
	
	   i=i+1
	
	ENDFOR
	
	END

Syntax for While:	**Example: Print n natural numbers**

WHILE (*condition*) DO
 	
   statement
 	
   ...
 	
ENDWHILE
	BEGIN GET n
	
	INITIALIZE i=1
	
	WHILE(i<=n) DO
	
	   PRINT i
	
	   i=i+1
	
	ENDWHILE
	
	END

Advantages:

- Pseudo is independent of any language; it can be used by most programmers.
- It is easy to translate pseudo code into a programming language.
- It can be easily modified as compared to flowchart.
- Converting a pseudo code to programming language is very easy as compared with converting a flowchart to programming language.

Disadvantages:

- It does not provide visual representation of the program's logic.

- There are no accepted standards for writing pseudo codes.
- It cannot be compiled nor executed.
- For a beginner, it is more difficult to follow the logic or write pseudo code as compared to flowchart.

Example

Addition of two numbers

BEGIN

GET a,b

ADD c=a+b

PRINT c

END

Algorithm	Flowchart	Pseudo code
An algorithm is a sequence of instructions used to solve a problem	It is a graphical representation of algorithm	It is a language representation of algorithm.
User needs knowledge to write algorithm.	not need knowledge of program to draw or understand flowchart	Not need knowledge of program language to understand or write a pseudo code.

1.4.3 Programming Language

A programming language is a set of symbols and rules for instructing a computer to perform specific tasks. The programmers have to follow all the specified rules before writing program using programming language. The user has to communicate with the computer using language which it can understand.

Types of programming language

- Machine language
- Assembly language
- High level language

Machine language

The computer can understand only machine language which uses 0's and 1's. In machine language the different instructions are formed by taking different combinations of 0's and 1's.

Advantages

Translation free:

Machine language is the only language which the computer understands. For executing any program written in any programming language, the conversion to machine language is necessary. The program written in machine language can be executed directly on computer. In this case any conversion process is not required.

High speed

The machine language program is translation free. Since the conversion time is saved, the execution of machine language program is extremely fast.

Disadvantage

- It is hard to find errors in a program written in the machine language.
- Writing program in machine language is a time-consuming process.

Machine dependent: According to architecture used, the computer differs from each other. So, machine language differs from computer to computer. So, a program developed for a particular type of computer may not run-on other type of computer.

Assembly language

- To overcome the issues in programming language and make the programming process easier, an assembly language is developed which is logically equivalent to machine language but it is easier for people to read, write and understand.
- Assembly language is symbolic representation of machine language. Assembly languages are symbolic programming language that uses symbolic notation to represent machine language instructions. They are called low level language because they are so closely related to the machines.
  Ex: ADD a, b

Assembler:

Assembler is the program which translates assembly language instruction in to a machine language.

Advantage:

- Easy to understand and use.
- It is easy to locate and correct errors.

Disadvantage

Machine dependent

The assembly language program which can be executed on the machine depends on the architecture of that computer.

Hard to learn

It is machine dependent, so the programmer should have the hardware knowledge to create applications using assembly language.

Less efficient

- Execution time of assembly language program is more than machine language program.

- Because assembler is needed to convert from assembly language to machine language.

High level language

High level language contains English words and symbols. The specified rules are to be followed while writing program in high level language. The interpreter or compilers are used for converting these programs in to machine readable form.

Translating high level language to machine language

The programs that translate high level language in to machine language are called interpreter or compiler.

Compiler:

A compiler is a program which translates the source code written in a high level language in to object code which is in machine language program. Compiler reads the whole program written in high level language and translates it to machine language. If any error is found it display error message on the screen.

Interpreter

Interpreter translates the high-level language program in line-by-line manner. The interpreter translates a high-level language statement in a source program to a machine code and executes it immediately before translating the next statement. When an error is found the execution of the program is halted and error message is displayed on the screen.

Advantages

Readability

High level language is closer to natural language so they are easier to learn and understand

Machine independent

High level language program has the advantage of being portable between machines.

Easy debugging

Easy to find and correct error in high level language

<u>Disadvantages</u>

Less efficient

The translation process increases the execution time of the program. Programs in high level language require more memory and take more execution time to execute.

<u>They are divided into following categories</u>

- Interpreted programming languages
- Functional programming languages
- Compiled programming languages
- Procedural programming languages
- Scripting programming language
- Markup programming language
- Concurrent programming language
- Object oriented programming language

Interpreted Programming Languages:

An interpreted language is a programming language for which most of its implementation executes instructions directly, without previously compiling a program into machine language instructions. The interpreter executes the program directly translating each statement into a sequence of one or more subroutines already compiled into machine code.

Examples: Pascal, Python

Functional programming language:

Functional programming language defines every computation as a mathematical evaluation. They focus on the programming languages are bound to mathematical calculations

Examples: Clean, Haskell

Compiled Programming language:

A compiled programming is a programming language whose implementation are typically compilers and not interpreters. It will produce a machine code from source code.

Examples: C, C++, C#, JAVA

Procedural programming language:

Procedural (imperative) programming implies specifying the steps that the programs should take to reach to an intended state. A procedure is a group of statements that can be referred through a procedure call. Procedures help in the reuse of code. Procedural programming makes the programs structured and easily traceable for program flow.

Examples: Hyper talk, MATLAB

Scripting language:

Scripting language are programming languages that control an application. Scripts can execute independent of any other application. They are mostly embedded in the application that they control and are used to automate frequently executed tasks like communicating with external program.

Examples: Apple script, VB script

Markup languages:

A markup language is an artificial language that uses annotations to text that define hoe the text is to be displayed.

Examples: HTML, XML

Concurrent programming language:

Concurrent programming is a computer programming technique that provides for the execution of operation concurrently, either with in a single computer or across a number of systems.

Examples: Joule, Limbo

Object oriented programming language:

Object oriented programming is a programming paradigm based on the concept of objects which may contain data in the form of procedures often known as methods.

Examples: Lava, Moto

1.5 ALGORITHMIC PROBLEM SOLVING:

Algorithmic problem solving is solving problem that require the formulation of an algorithm for the solution.

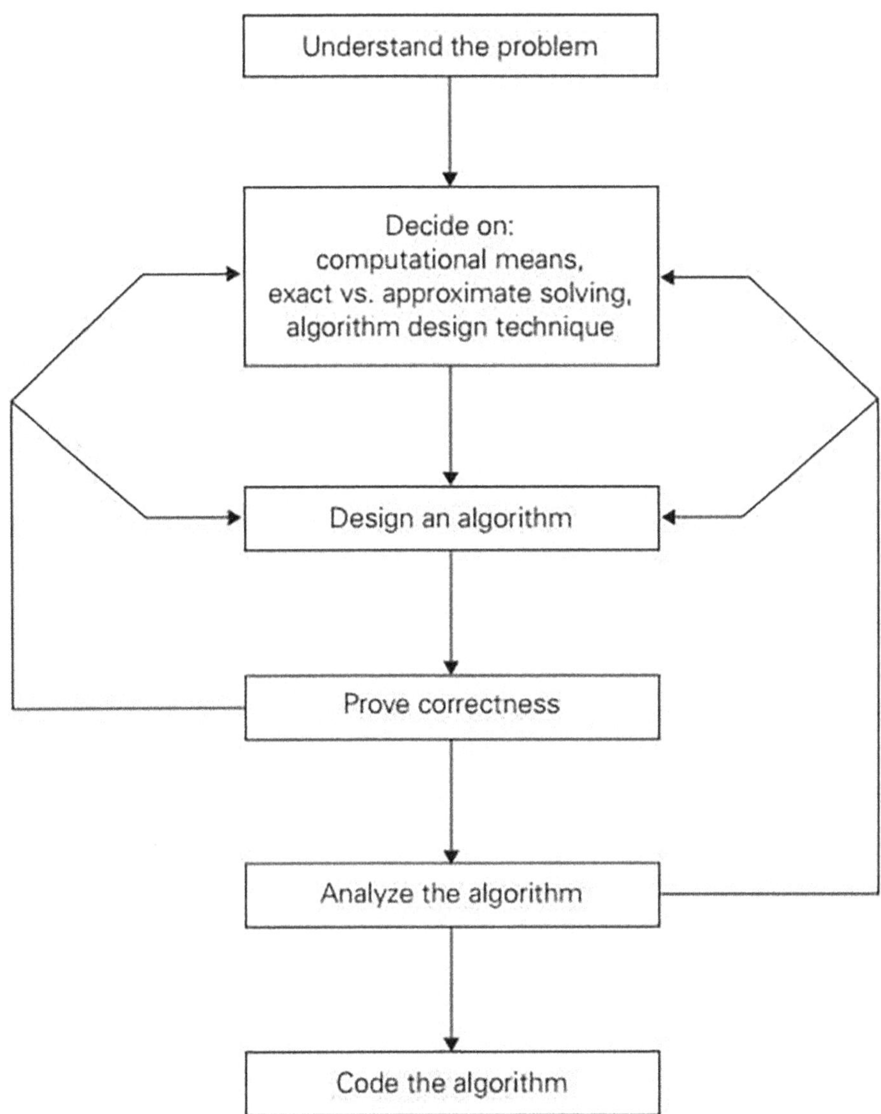

1.5.1 Understanding the Problem

- It is the process of finding the input of the problem that the algorithm solves.
- It is very important to specify exactly the set of inputs the algorithm needs to handle.

- A correct algorithm is not one that works most of the time, but one that works correctly for all legitimate inputs.

1.5.2 Ascertaining the Capabilities of the Computational Device

- If the instructions are executed one after another, it is called sequential algorithm.
- If the instructions are executed concurrently, it is called parallel algorithm.

1.5.3 Choosing between Exact and Approximate Problem Solving

- The next principal decision is to choose between solving the problem exactly or solving it approximately.
- Based on this, the algorithms are classified as exact algorithm and approximation algorithm.

1.5.4 Deciding a data structure

- Data structure plays a vital role in designing and analysis the algorithms.
- Some of the algorithm design techniques also depend on the structuring data specifying a problem's instance
- Algorithm+ Data structure=programs.

1.5.5 Algorithm Design Techniques

- An **algorithm design technique** (or "strategy" or "paradigm") is a general approach to solving problems algorithmically that is applicable to a variety of problems from different areas of computing.
- Learning these techniques is of utmost importance for the following reasons.
- First, they provide guidance for designing algorithms for new problems,
- Second, algorithms are the cornerstone of computer science

1.5.6 Methods of Specifying an Algorithm

- **Pseudocode** is a mixture of a natural language and programming language-like constructs. Pseudocode is usually more precise than natural language, and its usage often yields more succinct algorithm descriptions.
- In the earlier days of computing, the dominant vehicle for specifying algorithms was a **flowchart**, a method of expressing an algorithm by a collection of connected geometric shapes containing descriptions of the algorithm's steps.
- **Programming language** can be fed into an electronic computer directly. Instead, it needs to be converted into a computer program written in a particular computer language. We can look at such a program as yet another way of specifying the algorithm, although it is preferable to consider it as the algorithm's implementation.

1.5.7 Proving an Algorithm's Correctness

- Once an algorithm has been specified, you have to prove its correctness. That is, you have to prove that the algorithm yields a required result for every legitimate input in a finite amount of time.
- A common technique for proving correctness is to use mathematical induction because an algorithm's iterations provide a natural sequence of steps needed for such proofs.
- It might be worth mentioning that although tracing the algorithm's performance for a few specific inputs can be a very worthwhile activity, it cannot prove the algorithm's correctness conclusively. But in order to show that an algorithm is incorrect, you need just one instance of its input for which the algorithm fails.

1.5.8 Analyzing an Algorithm

1. Efficiency:

- ➢ Time efficiency, indicating how fast the algorithm runs,
- ➢ Space efficiency, indicating how much extra memory it uses.

2. Simplicity:

- ➢ An algorithm should be precisely defined and investigated with mathematical expressions.
- ➢ Simpler algorithms are easier to understand and easier to program.
- ➢ Simple algorithms usually contain fewer bugs.

1.5.9 Coding an Algorithm

- ➢ Most algorithms are destined to be ultimately implemented as computer programs. Programming an algorithm presents both a peril and an opportunity.
- ➢ A working program provides an additional opportunity in allowing an empirical analysis of the underlying algorithm. Such an analysis is based on timing the program on several inputs and then analyzing the results obtained.

1.6 SIMPLE STRATEGIES FOR DEVELOPING ALGORITHMS:

- Iterations
- Recursions

1.6.1 Iterations

A sequence of statements is executed until a specified condition is true is called iterations.

- for loop
- While loop

Syntax for For:	Example: Print n natural numbers

FOR (*start-value to end-value*) DO
 	
   statement
 	
   ...
 	
ENDFOR
	BEGIN GET n
	
	INITIALIZE i=1
	
	FOR (i<=n) DO
	
	   PRINT i
	
	   i=i+1
	
	ENDFOR
	
	END

Syntax for While:	Example: Print n natural numbers

WHILE (condition) DO
 	
   statement
 	
   ...
 	
ENDWHILE
	BEGIN
	
	GET n
	
	INITIALIZE i=1
	
	WHILE(i<=n) DO
	
	   PRINT i
	
	   i=i+1
	
	ENDWHILE
	
	END

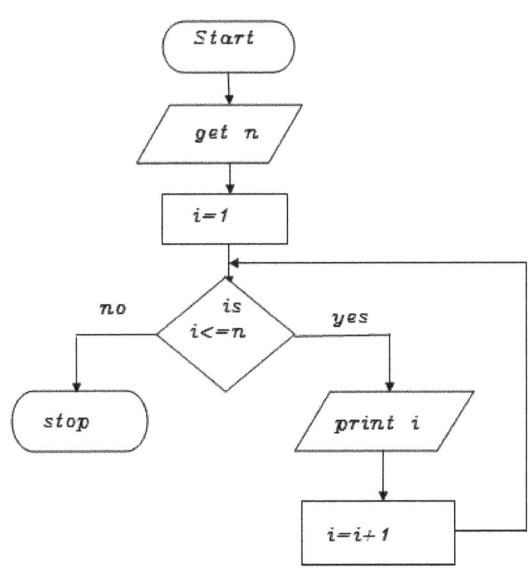

1.6.2 Recursions

- A function that calls itself is known as recursion.
- Recursion is a process by which a function calls itself repeatedly until some specified condition has been satisfied.

Algorithm for factorial of n numbers using recursion

Main function

Step1: Start

Step2: Get n

Step3: call factorial(n)

Step4: print fact

Step5: Stop

Sub function factorial(n)

Step1: if(n==1) then fact=1 return fact

Step2: else fact=n*factorial(n-1) and return fact

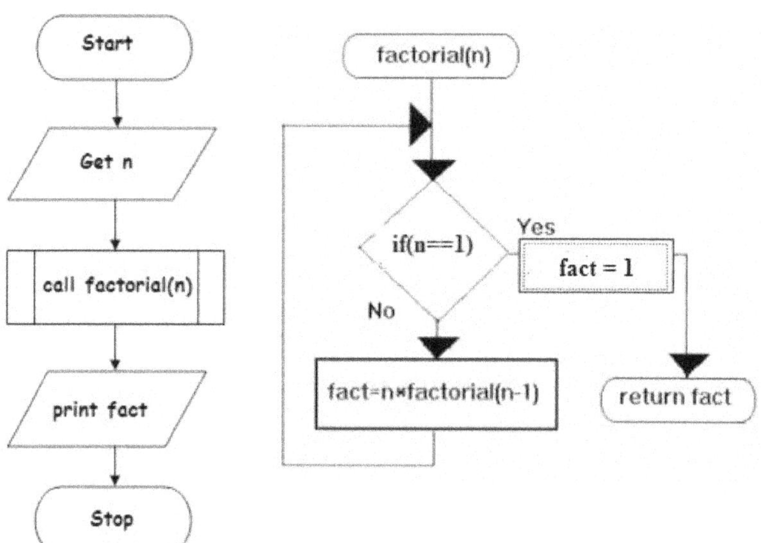

Pseudo code for factorial using recursion

Main function

BEGIN

GET n

CALL factorial(n)

PRINT fact

BIN

Sub function factorial(n)

IF(n==1) THEN

    fact=1

    RETURN fact

ELSE

    RETURN fact=n*factorial(n-1)

More examples

Write an algorithm to find area of a rectangle		
Step 1: Start	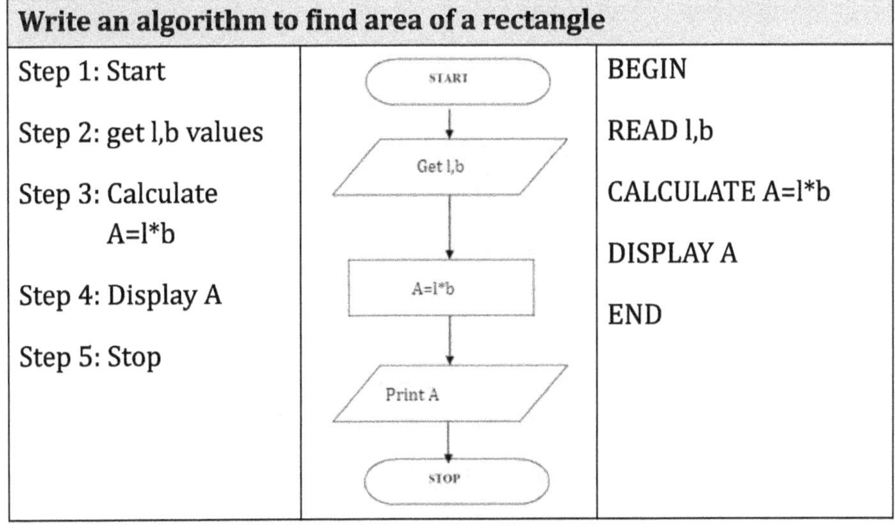	BEGIN
Step 2: get l,b values		READ l,b
Step 3: Calculate A=l*b		CALCULATE A=l*b
Step 4: Display A		DISPLAY A
Step 5: Stop		END

Write an algorithm for Calculating area and circumference of circle		
Step 1: Start Step 2: get r value Step 3: Calculate 　　A=3.14*r*r Step 4: Calculate 　　C=2.3.14*r Step 5: Display A,C Step 6: Stop	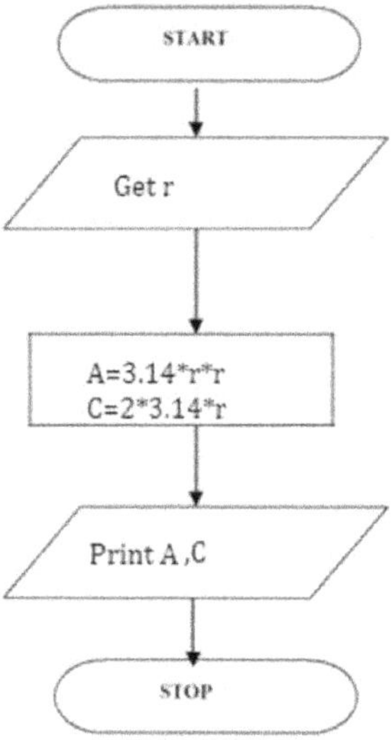 START Get r A=3.14*r*r C=2*3.14*r Print A ,C STOP	BEGIN READ r CALCULATE A and C A=3.14*r*r C=2*3.14*r DISPLAY A END

Write an algorithm for Calculating simple interest		
Step 1: Start Step 2: get P, n, r value Step3: Calculate 　　SI=(p*n*r)/100 Step 4: Display S Step 5: Stop	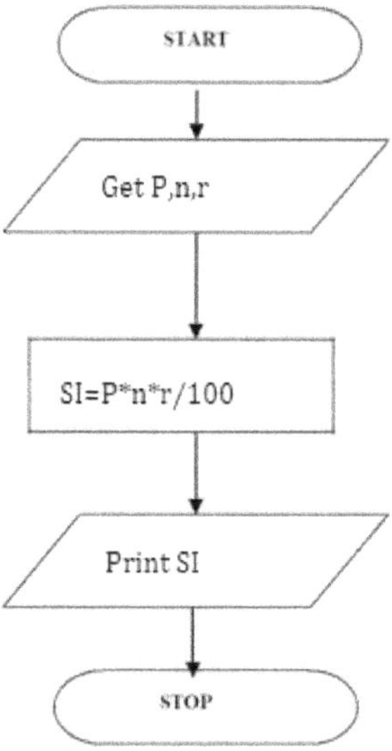 START Get P,n,r SI=P*n*r/100 Print SI STOP	BEGIN READ P, n, r CALCULATE S SI=(p*n*r)/100 DISPLAY SI END

Write an algorithm for Calculating engineering cutoff

Step 1: Start Step2: get P,C,M value Step3: calculate Cutoff= (P/4+C/4+M/2) Step 4: Display Cutoff Step 5: Stop	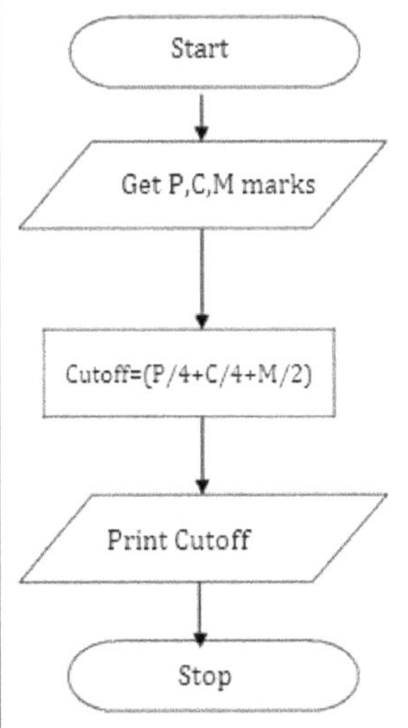	BEGIN READ P,C,M CALCULATE Cutoff= (P/4+C/4+M/2) DISPLAY Cutoff END

To check greatest of two numbers

Step 1: Start

Step 2: get a,b value

Step 3: check if(a>b) print a is greater Step 4: else b is greater

Step 5: Stop

BEGIN

READ a,b

IF (a>b) THEN

DISPLAY a is greater

ELSE

DISPLAY b is greater

END IF

END

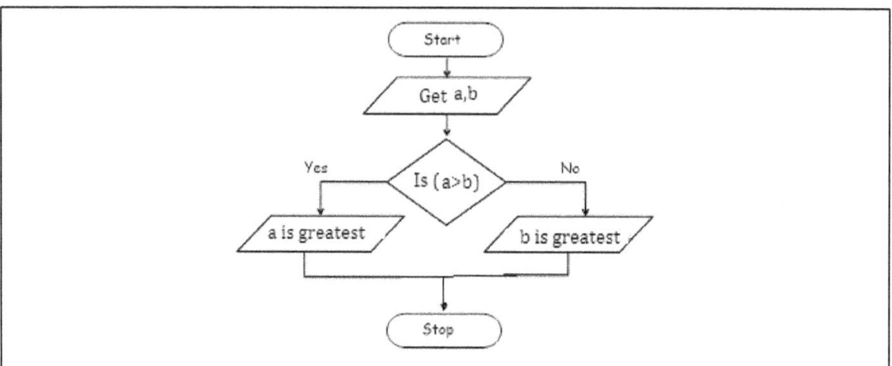

To check leap year or not

Step 1: Start Step 2: get y

Step 3: if(y%4==0) print leap year Step 4: else print not leap year

Step 5: Stop

BEGIN READ y

IF (y%4==0) THEN

DISPLAY leap year

ELSE

DISPLAY not leap year

END IF

END

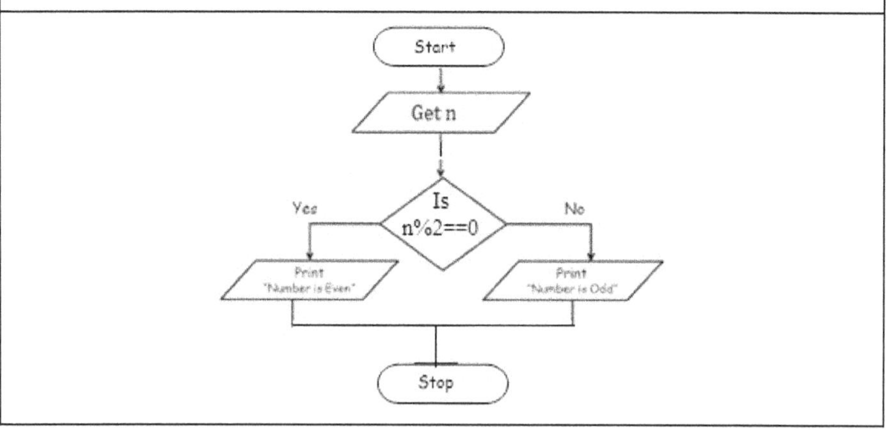

To check positive or negative number

Step 1: Start

Step 2: get num

Step 3: check if(num>0) print a is positive

Step 4: else num is negative

Step 5: Stop

BEGIN

READ num

IF (num>0) THEN

DISPLAY num is positive ELSE

DISPLAY num is negative END IF

END

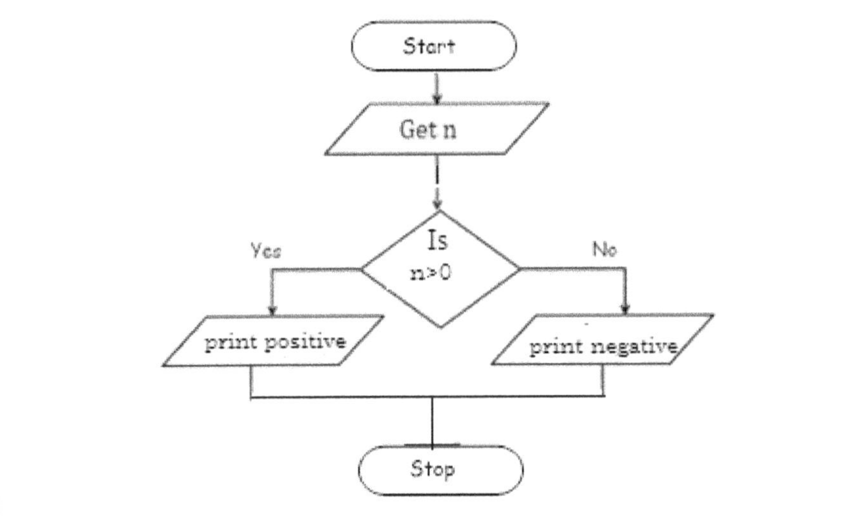

To check odd or even number
Step 1: Start Step 2: get num Step 3: check if(num%2==0) print num is even Step 4: else num is odd Step 5: Stop

BEGIN
 	
READ num
 	
IF (num%2==0) THEN
 	
DISPLAY num is even
 	
ELSE
 	
DISPLAY num is odd
 	
END IF
 	
END

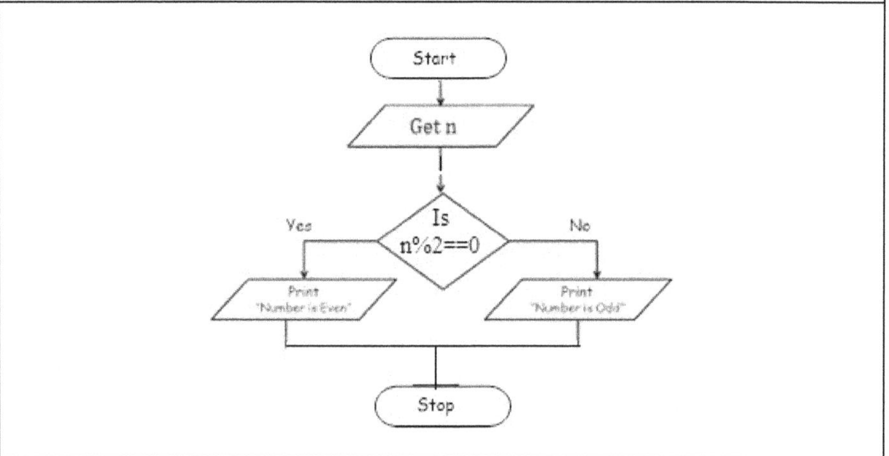

To check greatest of three numbers
Step1: Start Step2: Get A, B, C Step3: if(A>B) goto Step4 else goto step5 Step4: If(A>C) print A else print C Step5: If(B>C) print B else print C Step6: Stop

```
BEGIN

READ a, b, c

IF (a>b) THEN

   IF(a>c) THEN

        DISPLAY a is greater

   ELSE

        DISPLAY c is greater

   END IF

ELSE

   IF(b>c) THEN

   DISPLAY b is greater

   ELSE

   DISPLAY c is greater

   END IF

END IF

END
```

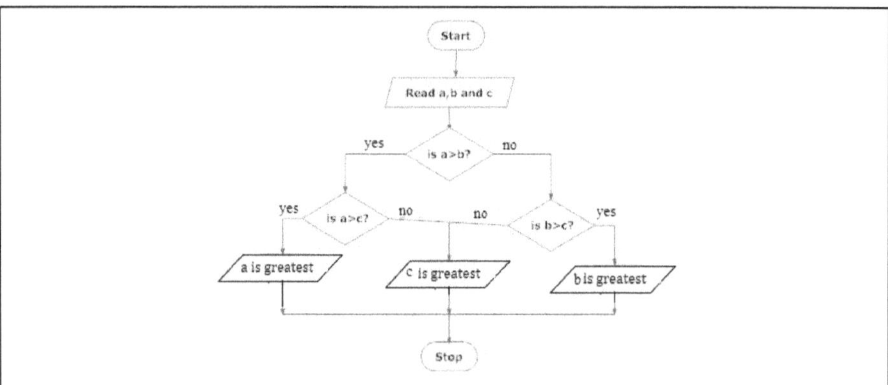

Write an algorithm to check whether given number is +ve, -ve or zero.

Step 1: Start

Step 2: Get n value.

Step 3: if (n ==0) print "Given number is Zero" Else goto step4

Step 4: if (n > 0) then Print "Given number is +ve"

Step 5: else Print "Given number is -ve"

Step 6: Stop

BEGIN

GET n

IF(n==0) THEN

   DISPLAY " n is zero"

ELSE

  IF(n>0) THEN

    DISPLAY "n is positive"

  ELSE

    DISPLAY "n is positive"

  END IF

END IF

END

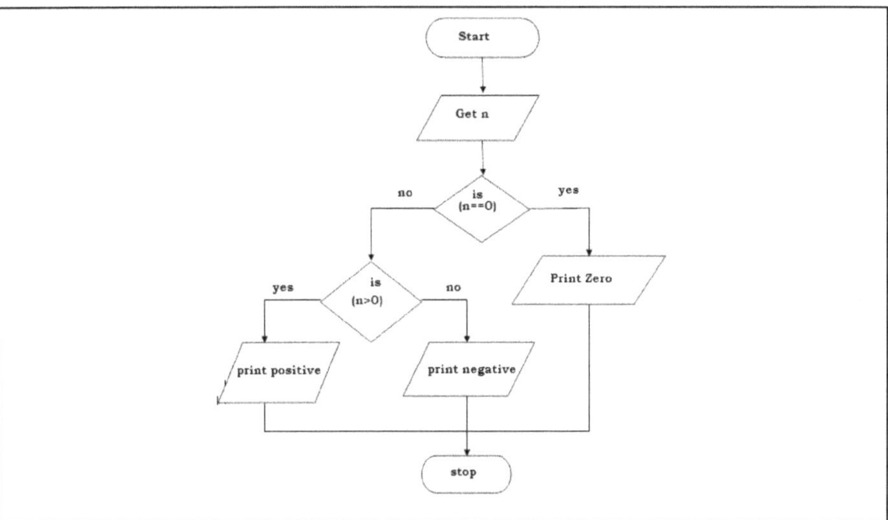

Write an algorithm to print all-natural numbers up to n

Step 1: Start

Step 2: get n value.

Step 3: initialize i=1

Step 4: if (i<=n) go to step 5 else go to step 8

Step 5: Print i value

step 6 : increment i value by 1

Step 7: go to step 4

Step 8: Stop

BEGIN

GET n

INITIALIZE i=1

WHILE(i<=n) DO

    PRINT i

    i=i+1

ENDWHILE

END

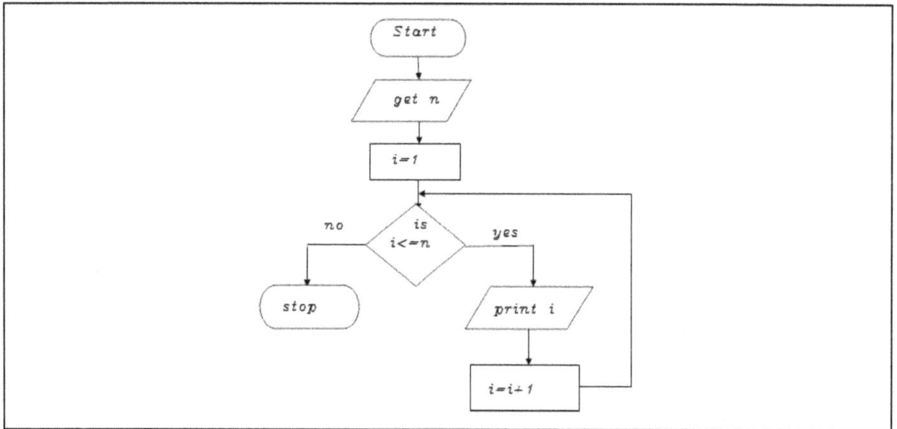

Write an algorithm to print n odd numbers

Step 1: start

Step 2: get n value

Step 3: set initial value i=1

Step 4: check if(i<=n) goto step 5 else goto step 8

step 5: print i value

Step 6: increment i value by 2

Step 7: goto step 4

Step 8: stop

BEGIN

GET n

INITIALIZE i=1

WHILE(i<=n) DO

   PRINT i

   i=i+2

ENDWHILE

END

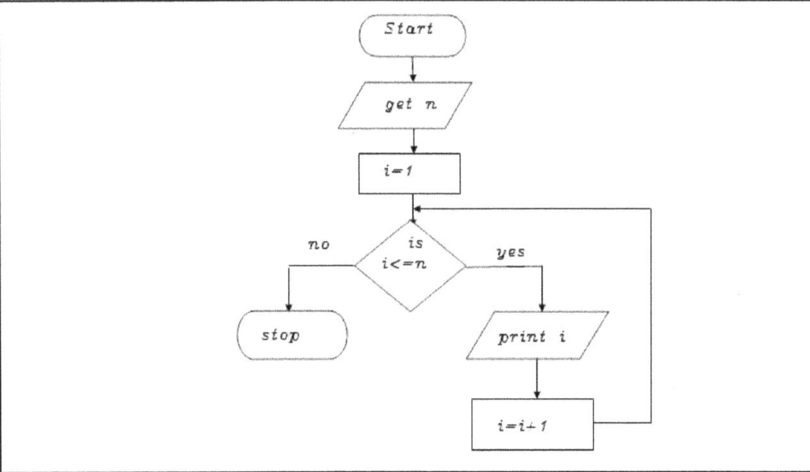

Write an algorithm to print n even numbers

Step 1: start

Step 2: get n value

Step 3: set initial value i=2

Step 4: check if(i<=n) goto step 5 else goto step8

Step 5: print i value

Step 6: increment i value by 2

Step 7: goto step 4

Step 8: stop

BEGIN

GET n

INITIALIZE i=2

WHILE(i<=n) DO

  PRINT i

  i=i+2

ENDWHILE

END

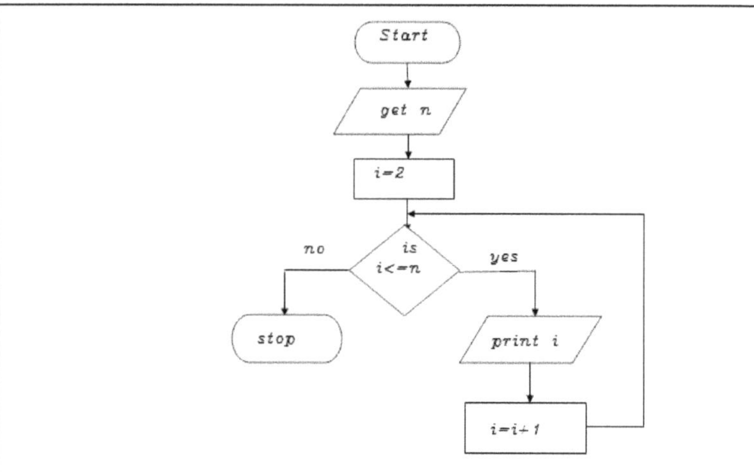

Write an algorithm to print squares of a number

Step 1: start

Step 2: get n value

Step 3: set initial value i=1

Step 4: check i value if(i<=n) goto step 5 else goto step8

Step 5: print i*i value

Step 6: increment i value by 1

Step 7: goto step 4

Step 8: stop

BEGIN GET n

INITIALIZE i=1

WHILE(i<=n) DO

   PRINT i*i

   i=i+1

ENDWHILE

END

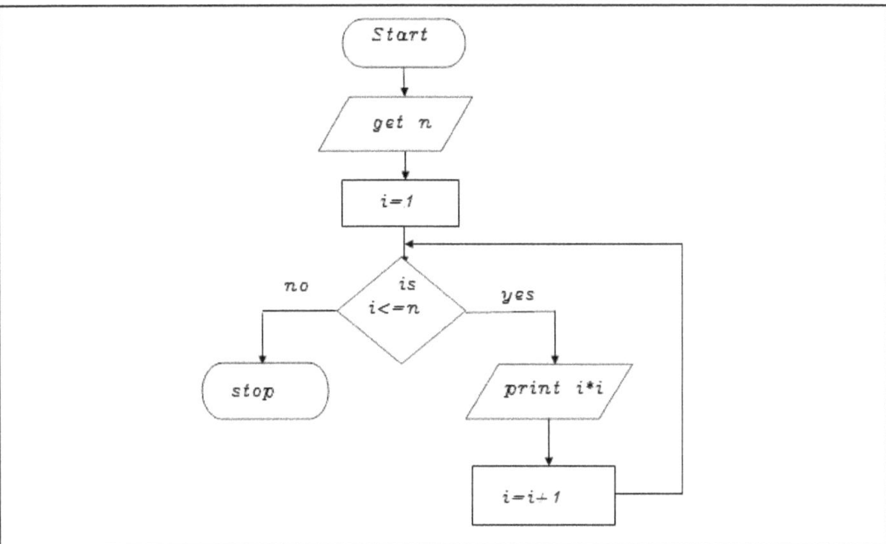

Write an algorithm to print to print cubes of a number

Step 1: start

Step 2: get n value

Step 3: set initial value i=1

Step 4: check i value if(i<=n) goto step 5 else goto step8

Step 5: print i*i *i value

Step 6: increment i value by 1

Step 7: goto step 4

Step 8: stop

```
BEGIN

GET n

INITIALIZE i=1

WHILE(i<=n) DO

    PRINT i*i*i

    i=i+1

ENDWHILE

END
```

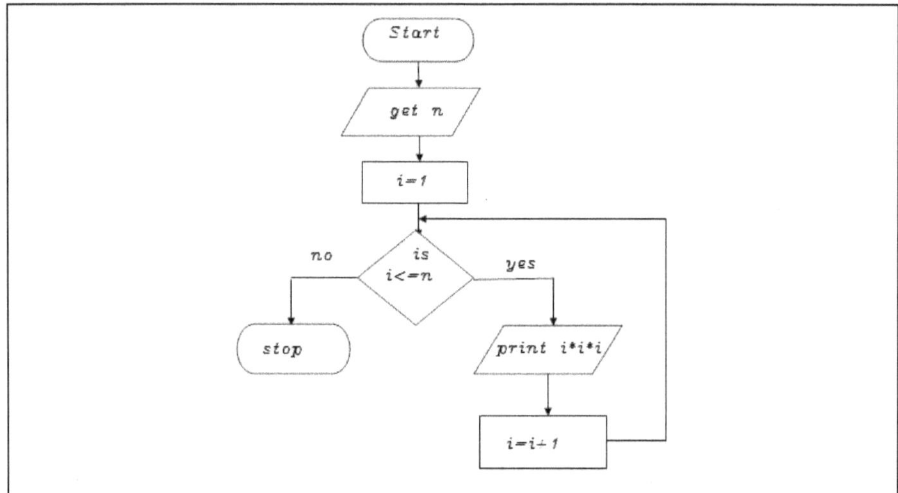

Write an algorithm to find sum of a given number

Step 1: start

Step 2: get n value

Step 3: set initial value i=1, sum=0

Step 4: check i value if(i<=n) goto step 5 else goto step8

Step 5: calculate sum=sum+i

step 6: increment i value by 1

Step 7: goto step 4

Step 8: print sum value

Step 9: stop

BEGIN

GET n

INITIALIZE i=1, sum=0

WHILE(i<=n) DO

    sum=sum+i i=i+1

ENDWHILE

PRINT sum

END

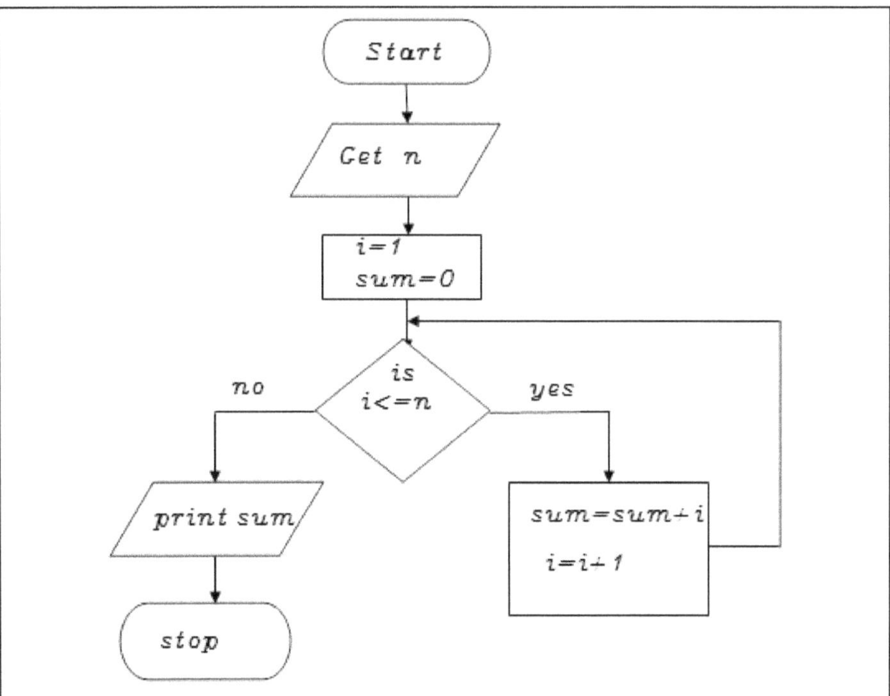

Write an algorithm to find factorial of a given number

Step 1: start

Step 2: get n value

Step 3: set initial value i=1, fact=1

Step 4: check i value if(i<=n) goto step 5 else goto step8

Step 5: calculate fact=fact*i

Step 6: increment i value by 1

Step 7: goto step 4

Step 8: print fact value

Step 9: stop

```
BEGIN

GET n

INITIALIZE i=1, fact=1

WHILE(i<=n) DO

    fact=fact*i

    i=i+1

ENDWHILE

PRINT fact

END
```

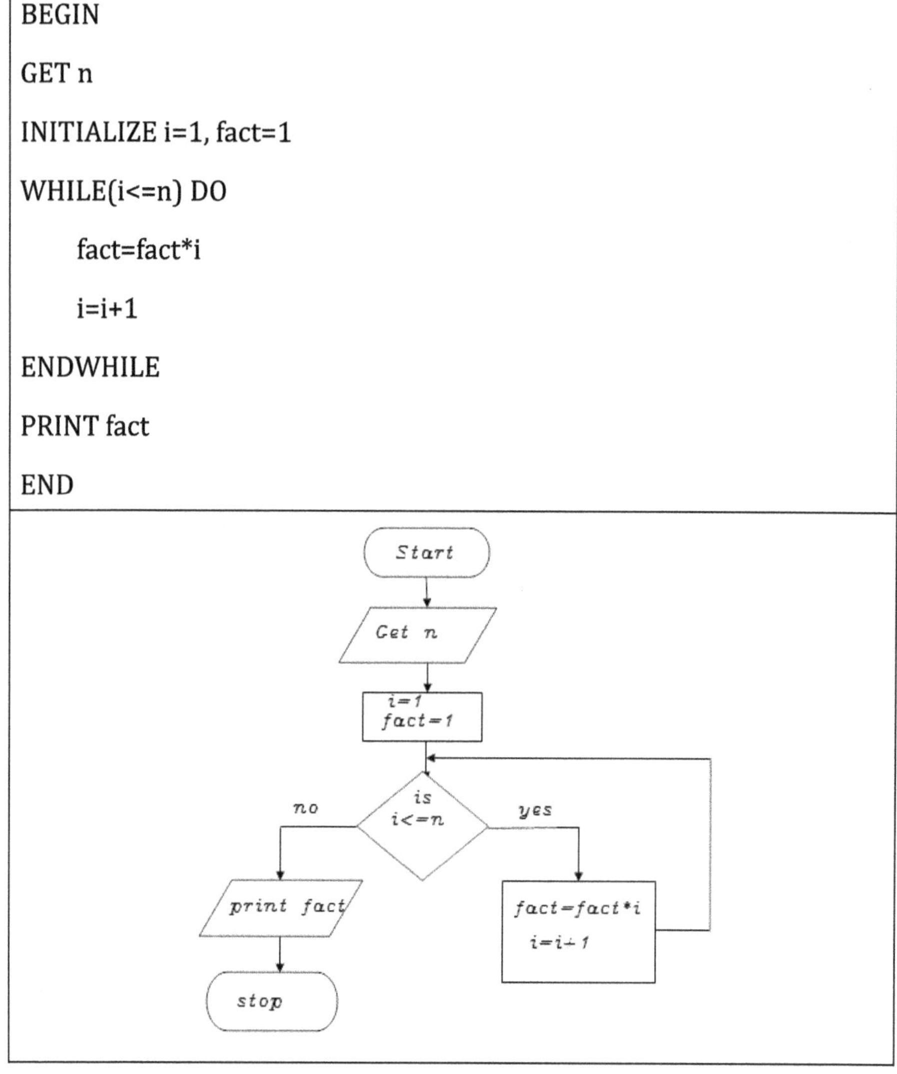

Illustrative problems:

Find minimum in a list:

ALGORITHM:

Step 1: Start the program.

Step 2: Get the list from the user.

Step 3: Assign min to a[1].

Step 4: Using for loop check for minimum value in list and assign to min.

Step 5: Display the minimum value.

Step 6: Stop the program.

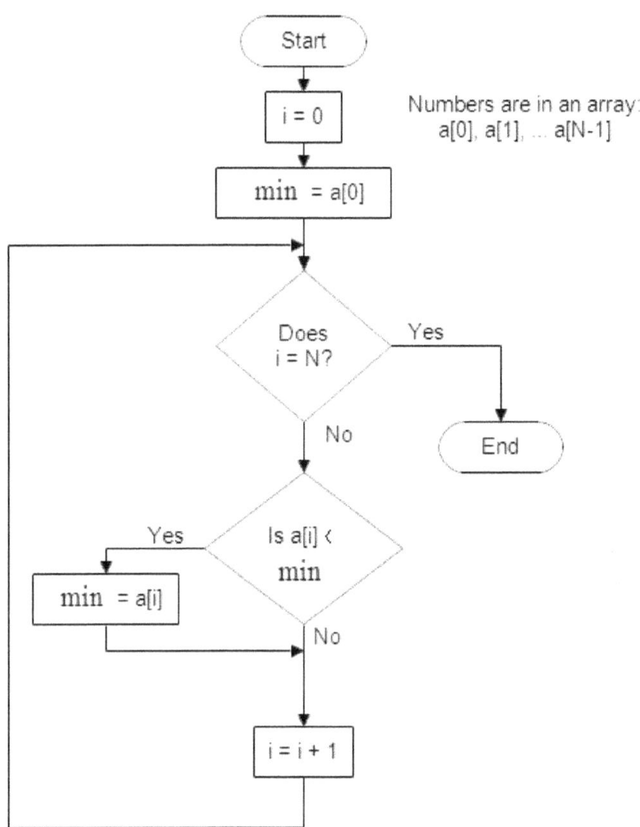

Insert a card in sorted list:

ALGORITHM:

Step 1: Start the program.

Step 2: Set the index value.

Step 3: Based on the index value insert the value in the list.

Step 4: Display the list.

Step 5: stop the program.

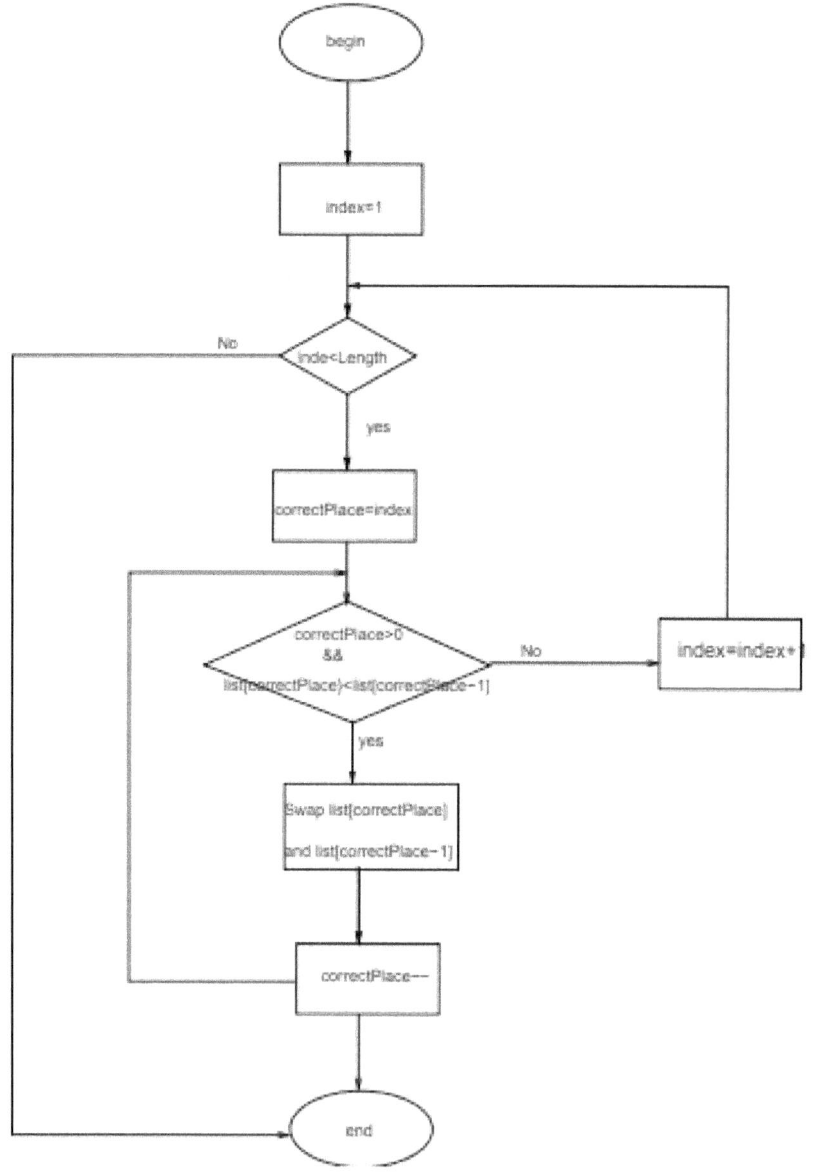

Guess a Number:

ALGORITHM:

Step 1: Start the program.

Step 2: Generate a random number.

Step 3: Get the number from the user.

Step 4: Check for guessing is right or not.

Step 5: If checking is right display the result guess is right else display whether it is too low or too high.

Step 6: Stop the program.

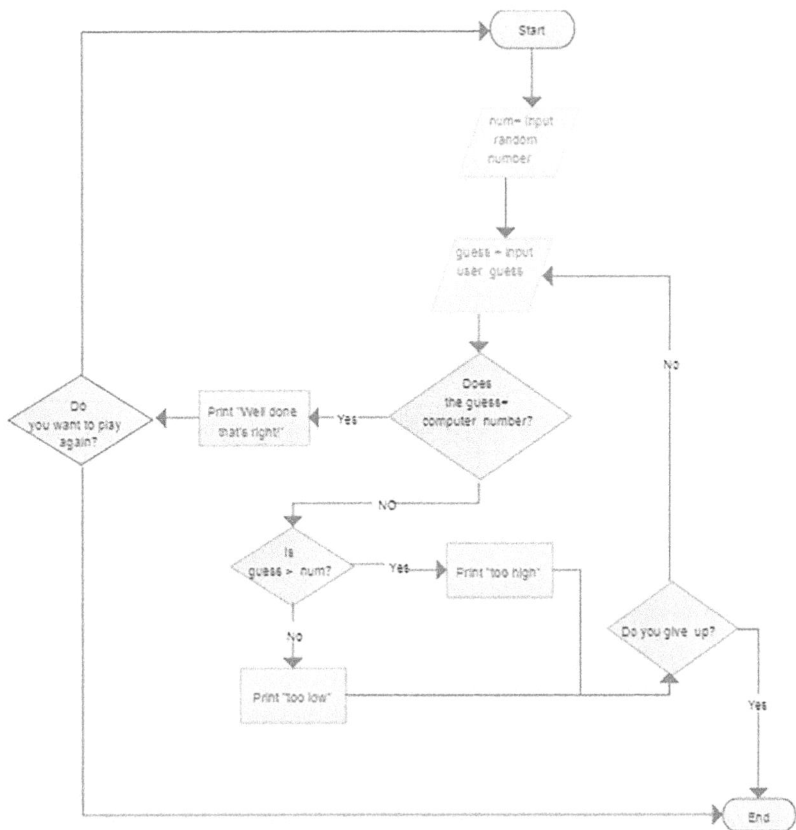

Tower of Hanoi:

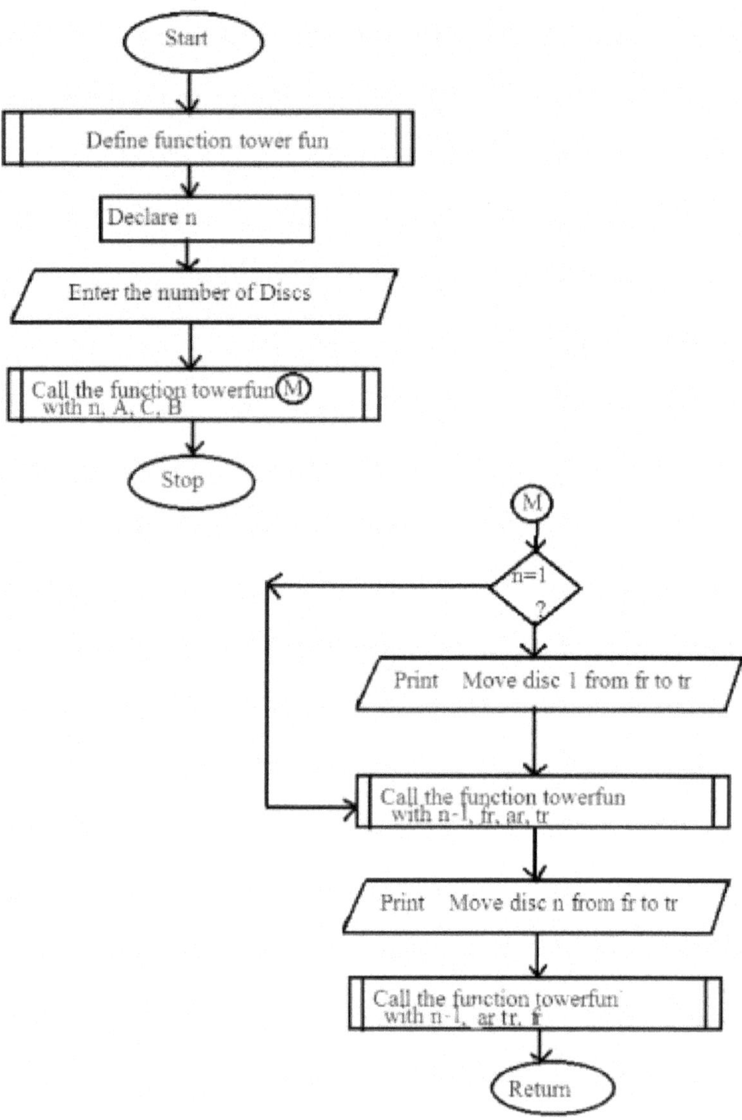

CHAPTER 2

INTRODUCTION TO PYTHON PROGRAMMING

Python interpreter and interactive mode, input and output functions; values and types: int, float, boolean, string, and list; variables, expressions, statements, tuple assignment, precedence of operators, comments; Modules and functions, function definition and use, flow of execution, parameters and arguments; Illustrative programs: exchange the values of two variables, circulate the values of n variables, distance between two points.

2.1 INTRODUCTION

Python is a general-purpose interpreted, interactive, object-oriented, and high- level programming language. It was created by Guido van Rossum during 1985- 1990. Python got its name from "Monty Python's flying circus". Python was released in the year 2000.

Python is a high-level, general-purpose programming language that is interpreted. Python's development model prioritizes readability of code, as shown by its extensive use of indentation. Its language structures and object-oriented style are aimed at assisting programmers in writing simple, logical code for both small and large-scale projects. It is described as **IIOOBL:**

- **Python is Interpreted**: Python is processed at runtime by the interpreter. You do not need to compile your program before executing it.

- **Python is Interactive**: You can actually sit at a Python prompt and interact with the interpreter directly to write your programs.
- **Python is Object-Oriented**: Python supports Object-Oriented style or technique of programming that encapsulates code within objects.
- **Python is a Beginner's Language**: Python is a great language for the beginner-level programmers and supports the development of a wide range of applications.

2.1.1 Python Features

- **Easy-to-learn:** Python is clearly defined and easily readable. The structure of the program is very simple. It uses few keywords.
- **Easy-to-maintain:** Python's source code is fairly easy-to-maintained.
- **Portable:** Python can run on a wide variety of hardware platforms and has the same interface on all platforms.
- **Interpreted:** Python is processed at runtime by the interpreter. So, there is no need to compile a program before executing it. You can simply run the program.
- **Extensible:** Programmers can embed python within their C, C++, Java Script, ActiveX, etc.
- **Free and Open Source:** Anyone can freely distribute it, read the source code, and edit it.
- **High Level Language:** When writing programs, programmers concentrate on solutions of the current problem, no need to worry about the low-level details.
- **Scalable:** Python provides a better structure and support for large programs than shell scripting.

2.1.2 Applications

- Bit Torrent file sharing
- Google search engine

- Youtube
- Intel, Cisco, HP, IBM
- i–Robot
- NASA
- Facebook
- Drop box etc.,

2.2 PYTHON INTERPRETER:

Interpreter: To execute a program in a high-level language by translating it one line at a time.

Compiler: To translate a program written in a high-level language into a low-level language all at once, in preparation for later execution.

COMPILER	INTERPRETER
Compiler Takes Entire program as input	Interpreter Takes Single instruction as input
Intermediate Object Code is generated	No Intermediate Object Code is generated
Conditional Control Statements are Executes faster	Conditional Control Statements are Executes slower
Memory Requirement is more (Since Object Code is Generated)	Memory Requirement is Less

COMPILER	INTERPRETER
Program need not be compiled every time	Every time higher level program is converted into lower-level program
Errors are displayed after entire program is checked	Errors are displayed for every instruction interpreted (if any)
Example: C Compiler	Example: PYTHON

2.2.1 <u>Modes of Python Interpreter</u>

Python Interpreter is a program that reads and executes Python code. It uses 2 modes of Execution.

- Interactive mode
- Script mode

Interactive mode:

Interactive Mode, as the name suggests, allows us to interact with OS. When we type Python statement, interpreter displays the result(s) immediately.

Advantages:

- Python, in interactive mode, is good enough to learn, experiment or explore.
- Working in interactive mode is convenient for beginners and for testing small pieces of code.

Drawback:

- We cannot save the statements and have to retype all the statements once again to re-run them.

In interactive mode, you type Python programs and the interpreter displays the result:

```
Python 3.7.6 Shell
File  Edit  Shell  Debug  Options  Window  Help
Python 3.7.6 (tags/v3.7.6:43364a7ae0,
42:30) [MSC v.1916 64 bit (AMD64)] on
Type "help", "copyright", "credits" or
more information.
>>> 1+1
2
>>>
```

The chevron, >>>, is the prompt the interpreter uses to indicate that it is ready for you to enter code. If you type 1 + 1, the interpreter replies 2.

```
Python 3.7.6 Shell
File  Edit  Shell  Debug  Options  Window  Help
Python 3.7.6 (tags/v3.7.6:43364
9, 00:42:30) [MSC v.1916 64 bit
2
Type "help", "copyright", "cred
)" for more information.
>>> print ('Hello, World!')
Hello, World!
>>> |
```

This is an example of a print statement. It displays a result on the screen. In this case, the result is the words.

```
Python 3.7.6 Shell                                    —   □   ×
File  Edit  Shell  Debug  Options  Window  Help
Python 3.7.6 (tags/v3.7.6:43364a7ae0, Dec 19 201
9, 00:42:30) [MSC v.1916 64 bit (AMD64)] on win3
2
Type "help", "copyright", "credits" or "license(
)" for more information.
>>> print ('Hello, World!')
Hello, World!
>>> a=3
>>> b=6
>>> c=a-b
>>> print(c)
-3
>>> 4**3
64
>>>

                                              Ln: 12  Col: 4
```

Script mode:

In script mode, we type python program in a file and then use interpreter to execute the content of the file. Scripts can be saved to disk for future use. Python scripts have the extension .py, meaning that the filename ends with .py. Save the code with filename.py and run the interpreter in script mode to execute the script.

Example:

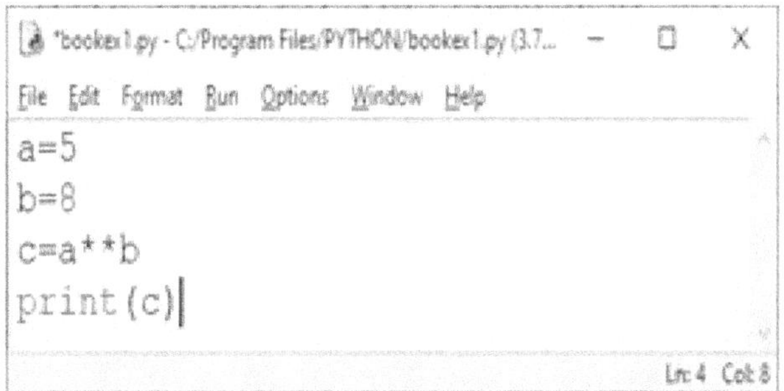


```
Python 3.7.6 Shell                                        —    □    X
File  Edit  Shell  Debug  Options  Window  Help
Python 3.7.6 (tags/v3.7.6:43364a7ae0, Dec 19 2019, 00:42:30) [M
SC v.1916 64 bit (AMD64)] on win32
Type "help", "copyright", "credits" or "license()" for more inf
ormation.
>>>
================= RESTART: C:/Program Files/PYTHON/bookex1.py
=================
390625
>>>
                                                          Ln: 3  Col: 0
```

Interactive mode	Script mode
A way of using the Python interpreter by typing commands and expressions at the prompt.	A way of using the Python interpreter to read and execute statements in a script.
In this mode, saving and editing the code is not possible	In this mode, saving and editing the code is possible
If we want to experiment with the code, we can use interactive mode.	If we are very clear about the code, we can use script mode.

we cannot save the statements for further use and we have to retype all the statements to re-run them.	we can save the statements for further use and we no need to retype all the statements to re-run them.
We can see the results immediately.	We can't see the result immediately.

2.3 INTEGRATED DEVELOPMENT LEARNING ENVIRONMENT (IDLE):

- It is a graphical user interface which is completely written in Python.
- It is bundled with the default implementation of the python language and also comes with optional part of the Python packaging.
- IDLE is designed to be a simple IDE that is appropriate for beginners, notably in an academic context. As a result, it is cross-platform and features-light.
- IDLE includes a full-featured text editor with syntax highlighting, autocompletion, and smart indent for writing Python scripts. There's even a debugger with stepping and breakpoints. This facilitates debugging.

2.3.1 Features of IDLE

- Multi-window text editor with syntax highlighting.
- Auto completion with smart indentation.
- Python shell with syntax highlighting.
- Stepping, persistent breakpoints, and call stack visibility are all included in the integrated debugger.
- Coded in 100% pure Python, using the tkinter GUI toolkit
- Search within any window, replace within editor windows, and search through multiple files (grep)

2.4 VALUES AND DATA TYPES:

- **Value:**

    - Value can be any letter, number or string.
    - Eg, Values are 2, 42.0, and 'Hello, World!'. (These values belong to different datatypes.)

- **Data type:**

    - Every value in Python has a data type.
    - It is a set of values, and the allowable operations on those values.
    - Python has 5 standard data types:

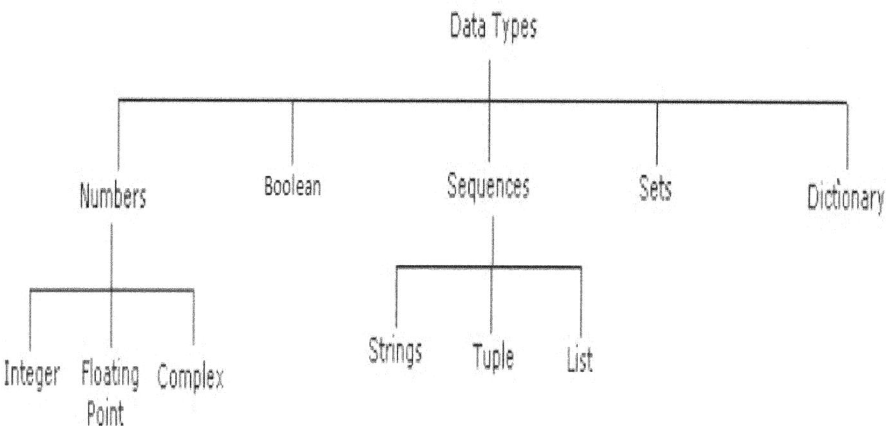

Numbers:

- Number data type stores Numerical Values.
- This data type is immutable [i.e. values/items cannot be changed].
- Python supports integers, floating point numbers and complex numbers. They are defined as,

Integers	Long	Float	Complex
- They are often called just integers or **int**. - They are positive or negative whole numbers with no decimal point.	-They are long integers. -They can also be represented in octal and hexadecimal representation.	-They are written with a decimal point dividing the integer and the fractional parts.	-They are of the form **a + bj**, where a and b are floats and j represents the square root of -1 (which is an imaginary number). -The real part of the number is a, and the imaginary part is b.
Eg, 56	Eg, 5692431L	Eg, 56.778	Eg, square root of -1 is a complex number

- **Sequence:**

  - A sequence is an ordered collection of items, indexed by positive integers.
  - It is a combination of mutable (value can be changed) and immutable (values cannot be changed) data types.
  - There are three types of sequence data type available in Python, they are

    - Strings
    - Lists
    - Tuples

  - **Strings**

    - ❖ A String in Python consists of a series or sequence of characters - letters, numbers, and special characters. Strings are marked by quotes:

      - ➤ single quotes (' ') Eg, 'This a string in single quotes'
      - ➤ double quotes (" ") Eg, "This a string in double quotes"
      - ➤ triple quotes (""" """) Eg, This is a paragraph. It is made up of multiple lines and sentences."""

❖ Individual character in a string is accessed using a subscript (index).

❖ Characters can be accessed using indexing and slicing operations

❖ Strings are immutable i.e. the contents of the string cannot be changed after it is created.

○ **Indexing:**

String A	H	E	L	L	O
Positive Index	0	1	2	3	4
Negative Index	-5	-4	-3	-2	-1

➢ Positive indexing helps in accessing the string from the beginning

➢ Negative subscript helps in accessing the string from the end.

➢ Subscript 0 or –ve n (where n is length of the string) displays the first element.

```
Python 3.7.6 Shell                        —    □    ×

File  Edit  Shell  Debug  Options  Window  Help
Python 3.7.6 (tags/v3.7.6:43364a7ae0,
Dec 19 2019, 00:42:30) [MSC v.1916 64
bit (AMD64)] on win32
Type "help", "copyright", "credits" o
r "license()" for more information.
>>> s="HELLO"
>>> s[0]
'H'
>>> s[-5]
'H'
>>> s[4]
'O'
>>> s[-1]
'O'
                              Ln: 12   Col: 4
```

Operations performed on strings:

- ➢ Indexing
- ➢ Slicing
- ➢ Concatenation
- ➢ Repetitions
- ➢ Member ship

Creating a string	>>> s="good morning"	Creating the list with elements of different data types.

Indexing	>>> print(s[2])
	
	o
	
	>>> print(s[6])
	
	o
		Accessing the item in the position 2
		
		Accessing the item in the position 6

Slicing (ending position -1)	>>> print(s[2:]) od morning	Displaying items from 2nd till last.
Slice operator is used to extract part of a data type	>>> print(s[:4]) Good	Displaying items from 1st position till 3rd
Concatenation	>>>print(s+"friends") good morningfriends	-Adding and printing the characters of two strings.
Repetition	>>>print(s*2) good morninggood morning	Creates new strings, concatenating multiple copies of the same string

in, not in (membership operator)	>>> s="good morning"
	>>>"m" in s True
	>>> "a" not in s
	True
		Using membership operators to check a particular character is in string or not. Returns true if present.

- ○ **Lists**

  - ❖ List is an ordered sequence of items. Values in the list are called elements/items.
  - ❖ It can be written as a list of comma-separated items (values) between square brackets [ ].
  - ❖ Items in the lists can be of different data types.
  - ❖ **Operations on list:** Indexing Slicing Concatenation Repetitions Updation, Insertion, Deletion

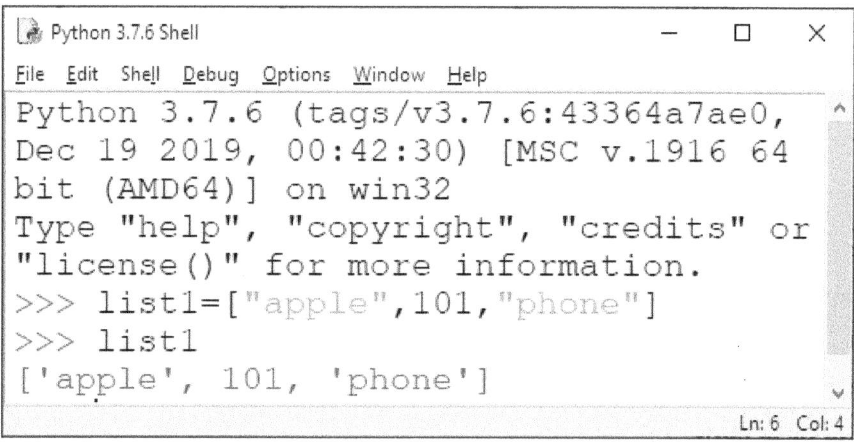

Creating a list	>>>list1=["python", 7.79, 101, "hello"] >>>list2=["god",6.78,9]	Creating the list with elements of different data types.
Indexing	>>>print(list1[0]) python >>> list1[2] 101	Accessing the item in the position 0 Accessing the item in the position 2

Slicing (ending position -1) Slice operator is used to extract part of a string, or some part of a list Python	>>> print(list1[1:3]) [7.79, 101] >>>print(list1[1:]) [7.79, 101, 'hello']	Displaying items from 1st till 2nd. Displaying items from 1st position till last.
Concatenation	>>>print(list1+list2) ['python', 7.79, 101, 'hello', 'god', 6.78, 9]	Adding and printing the items of two lists.

Repetition	>>> list2*3 ['god', 6.78, 9, 'god', 6.78, 9, 'god', 6.78, 9]	Creates new strings, concatenating multiple copies of the same string
Updating the list	>>> list1[2]=45 >>>print(list1) ['python', 7.79, 45, 'hello']	Updating the list using index value

Inserting an element	>>> list1.insert(2,"program")
	>>> print(list1)
	['python', 7.79, 'program', 45, 'hello']
		Inserting an element in 2nd position

Removing an element	>>> list1.remove(45)
	>>> print(list1)
	['python', 7.79, 'program', 'hello']
		Removing an element by giving the element directly

- o **Tuple:**

    - ❖ A tuple is same as list, except that the set of elements is enclosed in parentheses () instead of square brackets [].

- ❖ A tuple is an immutable list. i.e., once a tuple has been created, you can't add elements to a tuple or remove elements from the tuple.
- ❖ Tuple items are ordered, unchangeable, and allow duplicate values.
- ❖ Tuple items are indexed, the first item has index [0], the second item has index [1] etc.

❖ **Benefit of Tuple:**

- ➢ Tuples are faster than lists.
- ➢ If the user wants to protect the data from accidental changes, tuple can be used.
- ➢ Tuples can be used as keys in dictionaries, while lists can't.

```
Python 3.7.6 Shell                                    —  □  X
File  Edit  Shell  Debug  Options  Window  Help
Python 3.7.6 (tags/v3.7.6:43364a7ae0, Dec 19 2019
, 00:42:30) [MSC v.1916 64 bit (AMD64)] on win32
Type "help", "copyright", "credits" or "license()
" for more information.
>>> tuple1=("apple",1.2,"computer",45,236)
>>> tuple1
('apple', 1.2, 'computer', 45, 236)
                                          Ln: 6  Col: 4
```

❖ **Basic Operations:**

- ➢ Creation
- ➢ Indexing
- ➢ Slicing
- ➢ Concatenation
- ➢ Repetition

Creating a tuple	>>>t=("python", 7.79, 101, "hello")	Creating the tuple with elements of different data types.
Indexing	>>>print(t[0]) python >>> t[2] 101	Accessing the item in the position 0 Accessing the item in the position 2
Slicing(ending position -1)	>>>print(t[1:3]) (7.79, 101)	Displaying items from 1st till 2nd.
Concatenation	>>> t+("ram", 67) ('python', 7.79, 101, 'hello', 'ram', 67)	Adding tuple elements at the end of another tuple elements
Repetition	>>>print(t*2) ('python', 7.79, 101, 'hello', 'python', 7.79, 101, 'hello')	Creates new strings, concatenating multiple copies of the same string

❖ Altering the tuple data type leads to error. Following error occurs when user tries to do.

```
Python 3.7.6 Shell                                        —   □   ×
File  Edit  Shell  Debug  Options  Window  Help
Type  "help",  "copyright",  "credits"  or  "license()"
"  for  more  information.
>>> tuple1=("apple",1.2,"computer",45,236)
>>> tuple1
('apple', 1.2, 'computer', 45, 236)
>>> tuple1[1]=1
Traceback (most recent call last):
  File "<pyshell#2>", line 1, in <module>
    tuple1[1]=1
TypeError: 'tuple' object does not support item a
ssignment
>>>
                                              Ln: 11  Col: 4
```

- ○ **Mapping:**

  - ❖ This data type is unordered and mutable.
  - ❖ Dictionaries fall under Mappings.
  - ❖ Dictionaries:

    - ➤ Lists are ordered sets of objects, whereas dictionaries are unordered sets.
    - ➤ Dictionary is created by using curly brackets. i,e. {}
    - ➤ Dictionaries are accessed via keys and not via their position.
    - ➤ A dictionary is an associative array (also known as hashes). Any key of the dictionary is associated (or mapped) to a value.
    - ➤ The values of a dictionary can be any Python data type. So, dictionaries are unordered key-value-pairs (The association of a key and a value is called a key- value pair)
    - ➤ Dictionaries don't support the sequence operation of the sequence data types like strings, tuples and lists.

```
Python 3.7.6 Shell                                    —    □    X
File  Edit  Shell  Debug  Options  Window  Help
Python 3.7.6 (tags/v3.7.6:43364a7ae0, Dec 19 2019
, 00:42:30) [MSC v.1916 64 bit (AMD64)] on win32
Type "help", "copyright", "credits" or "license()
" for more information.
>>> data={"Name":"JOE","age":45,"degree":"Ph.D"}
>>> data
{'Name': 'JOE', 'age': 45, 'degree': 'Ph.D'}
                                                Ln: 6  Col: 4
```

Creating a dictionary	>>> food = {"ham":"yes", "egg" : "yes", "rate":450 } >>>print(food) {'rate': 450, 'egg': 'yes', 'ham': 'yes'}	Creating the dictionary with elements of different data types.
Indexing	>>>> print(food["rate"]) 450	Accessing the item with keys.
Slicing(ending position -1)	>>>print(t[1:3]) (7.79, 101)	Displaying items from 1st till 2nd.

If you try to access a key which doesn't exist, you will get an error message:

```
Python 3.7.6 Shell                                          —    □    ×
File  Edit  Shell  Debug  Options  Window  Help
"  for more information.
>>> data={"Name":"JOE","age":45,"degree":"Ph.D"}
>>> data
{'Name': 'JOE', 'age': 45, 'degree': 'Ph.D'}
>>> data["DOB"]
Traceback (most recent call last):
  File "<pyshell#2>", line 1, in <module>
    data["DOB"]
KeyError: 'DOB'
>>> |
                                                      Ln: 11  Col: 4
```

Data type	Compile time	Run time
int	a=10	a=int(input("enter a"))
float	a=10.5	a=float(input("enter a"))
string	a="panimalar"	a=input("enter a string")
list	a=[20,30,40,50]	a=list(input("enter a list"))
tuple	a=(20,30,40,50)	a=tuple(input("enter a tuple"))

2.5 VARIABLES, KEYWORDS EXPRESSIONS, STATEMENTS, COMMENTS, DOCSTRING, LINES AND INDENTATION, QUOTATION IN PYTHON, TUPLE ASSIGNMENT:

2.5.1 Variables

- A variable allows us to store a value by assigning it to a name, which can be used later.
- Named memory locations to store values.
- Programmers generally choose names for their variables that are meaningful.
- It can be of any length. No space is allowed.
- We don't need to declare a variable before using it. In Python, we simply assign a value to a variable and it will exist.

- **Assigning value to variable:**

  - ❖ Value should be given on the right side of assignment operator (=) and variable on left side.

```
>>>c=100
>>> print(c)
100
```

  - ❖ Assigning a single value to several variables simultaneously:

```
>>>a=b=c=10
>>> print(a,b,c)
10 10 10
```

  - ❖ Assigning multiple values to multiple variables:

```
>>>a,b,c=100,"world",2.5
>>> print(a,b,c)
100 world 2.5
```

2.5.2 Keywords

- Keywords are the reserved words in Python.
- We cannot use a keyword as variable name, function name or any other identifier.
- They are used to define the syntax and structure of the Python language.
- Keywords are case sensitive.

False	class	finally	is	return
None	continue	for	lambda	try
True	def	from	nonlocal	while
and	del	global	not	with
as	elif	if	or	yield
assert	else	import	pass	
break	except	in	raise	

2.5.3 Identifiers

- Identifier is the name given to entities like class, functions, variables etc. in Python.
- Identifiers can be a combination of letters in lowercase (a to z) or uppercase (A to Z) or digits (0 to 9) or an underscore (_).
- An identifier cannot start with a digit.
- Keywords cannot be used as identifiers.
- Cannot use special symbols like !, @, #, $, % etc. in our identifier.
- Identifier can be of any length.

Valid declarations	Invalid declarations
Num	Number 1
num	num 1
Num1	addition of program
_NUM	1Num
NUM_temp2	Num.no
IF	if
Else	else

2.5.4 Statements and Expressions

- **Statements:**

    - ❖ Instructions that a Python interpreter can executes are called statements.
    - ❖ A statement is a unit of code like creating a variable or displaying a value.
    - ❖ Here, the first line is an assignment statement that gives a value to n
    - ❖ The second line is a print statement that displays the value of n.

- **Expressions:**

    - ❖ An expression is a combination of values, variables, and operators.
    - ❖ A value all by itself is considered an expression, and also a variable.
    - ❖ So, the following are all legal expressions:

    ```
    >>> n = 17

    >>> print(n)
    ```

2.5.5 Input and Output

Input Functions:

Using input():

- ❖ In Python, we use input() function to take input from the user. Whatever you enter as input, the input function converts it into a string.

❖ Whatever you enter as input, the input function converts it into a string. If you enter an integer value still input() function convert it into a string.

Syntax:

Input(prompt)

```
Python 3.7.6 Shell                                    —    □    ×
File  Edit  Shell  Debug  Options  Window  Help
>>> x = input('Enter your name:')
Enter your name:JASON
>>> print('Hello, ' + x)
Hello, JASON
>>> |
                                                    Ln: 14  Col: 4
```

```
Python 3.7.6 Shell                                    —    □    ×
File  Edit  Shell  Debug  Options  Window  Help
>>> y=input("Enter the age:")
Enter the age:30
>>> y
'30'
                                                    Ln: 7  Col: 4
```

Output Functions:

Using print():

❖ The print() function prints the specified message to the screen, or other standard output device.

❖ The message can be a string, or any other object, the object will be converted into a string before written to the screen.

Syntax

```
print(object(s), sep=separator, end=end, file=file, flush=flush)
```

Parameter Values

Parameter	Description
object(s)	Any object, and as many as you like. Will be converted to string before printed
sep='separator'	Optional. Specify how to separate the objects, if there is more than one. Default is ' '
end='end'	Optional. Specify what to print at the end. Default is '\n' (line feed)
file	Optional. An object with a write method. Default is sys.stdout
flush	Optional. A Boolean, specifying if the output is flushed (True) or buffered (False). Default is False

```
Python 3.7.6 Shell                                          —    □    X

File  Edit  Shell  Debug  Options  Window  Help
>>> x = input('Enter your name:')
Enter your name:JASON
>>> print('Hello, ' + x)
Hello, JASON
>>>

                                                            Ln: 14  Col: 4
```

2.5.6 Comments

- A hash sign (#) is the beginning of a comment.
- Anything written after # in a line is ignored by interpreter.
- Eg: percentage = (minute * 100)/60 # calculating percentage of an hour
- Python does not have multiple-line commenting feature. You have to comment each line individually as follows:

Example:

This is a comment.

This is a comment, too.

I said that already.

2.5.7 DOCSTRING

- Docstring is short for documentation string.
- It is a string that occurs as the first statement in a module, function, class, or method definition. We must write what a function/class does in the docstring.
- Triple quotes are used while writing docstrings.

> **Syntax:**
> **functionname__doc.__**
> **Example:**

```
def double(num):
    """Function to double the value"""
    return 2*num
>>> print(double.__doc__)
Function to double the value
```

2.5.8 Lines and Indentation

- Most of the programming languages like C, C++, Java use braces { } to define a block of code. But python uses indentation.
- Blocks of code are denoted by line indentation.
- It is a space given to the block of codes for class and function definitions or flow control.

Example:

```
a=3
b=1
if a>b:
    print("a is greater")
else:
    print("b is greater")
```

2.6 QUOTATIONS IN PYTHON:

- Python accepts single ('), double (") and triple (''' or """) quotes to denote string literals.

- Anything that is represented using quotations are considered as string.
- single quotes ('   ') Eg, 'This a string in single quotes'
- double quotes (" ") Eg, "This a string in double quotes"
- triple quotes ("""   """) Eg, """This is a paragraph. It is made up of multiple lines and sentences."""

2.7 TUPLE ASSIGNMENT:

- An assignment to all of the elements in a tuple using a single assignment statement.
- Python has a very powerful tuple assignment feature that allows a tuple of variables on the left of an assignment to be assigned values from a tuple on the right of the assignment.
- The left side is a tuple of variables; the right side is a tuple of values.
- Each value is assigned to its respective variable.
- All the expressions on the right side are evaluated before any of the assignments. This feature makes tuple assignment quite versatile.
- Naturally, the number of variables on the left and the number of values on the right have to be the same.

```
Python 3.7.6 Shell                                          —    □    X
File  Edit  Shell  Debug  Options  Window  Help
Python 3.7.6 (tags/v3.7.6:43364a7ae0, Dec 19 2019, 00:42:30
) [MSC v.1916 64 bit (AMD64)] on win32
Type "help", "copyright", "credits" or "license()" for more
information.
>>> (a,b,c,d)=(1,2,3,4)
>>> a
1
>>> (a,b,c,d)=(1,2,3)
Traceback (most recent call last):
  File "<pyshell#2>", line 1, in <module>
    (a,b,c,d)=(1,2,3)
ValueError: not enough values to unpack (expected 4, got 3)
                                                        Ln: 11  Col: 4
```

Example:

- o It is useful to swap the values of two variables. With conventional assignment statements, we have to use a temporary variable. For example, to swap a and b:

Swap two numbers	Output:
a=2;b=3 print(a,b) temp = a a = b b = temp print(a,b)	 >>>(2, 3) >>>(3, 2)

- o Tuple assignment solves this problem neatly:

```
(a, b) = (b, a)
```

- o One way to think of tuple assignment is as tuple packing/ unpacking.

- ❖ In tuple packing, the values on the left are 'packed' together in a tuple:

```
>>> b = ("George", 25, "20000")   # tuple packing
```

- ❖ In tuple unpacking, the values in a tuple on the right are 'unpacked' into the variables/names on the right:

```
>>> b = ("George", 25, "20000")     # tuple packing
>>> (name, age, salary) = b   # tuple unpacking
>>> name
'George'
>>> age
25
>>> salary
'20000'
```

❖ The right side can be any kind of sequence (string, list, tuple)

Example:

-To split an email address in to user name and a domain

```
>>> mailid='god@abc.org'
>>> name,domain=mailid.split('@')
>>> print name
god
>>> print (domain)
abc.org
```

2.8 OPERATORS

○ Operators are the constructs which can manipulate the value of operands.

○ Consider the expression 4 + 5 = 9. Here, 4 and 5 are called operands and + is called operator

○ **Types of Operators:**

❖ Python language supports the following types of operators

- Arithmetic Operators
- Comparison (Relational) Operators
- Assignment Operators
- Logical Operators
- Bitwise Operators
- Membership Operators
- Identity Operators

❖ **Arithmetic operators:**

They are used to perform mathematical operations like addition, subtraction, multiplication etc. Assume, a=10 and b=5

Operator	Description	Example
+ Addition	Adds values on either side of the operator.	a + b = 20
- Subtraction	Subtracts right hand operand from left hand operand.	a – b = -5
* Multiplication	Multiplies values on either side of the operator	a * b = 50
/ Division	Divides left hand operand by right hand operand	a / b = 2.0
% Modulus	Divides left hand operand by right hand operand and returns remainder	a % b = 0
** Exponent	Performs exponential (power) calculation on operators	a**b =100000
//	Floor Division - The division of operands where the result is the quotient in which the digits after the decimal point are removed	a//b=2

```
Python 3.7.6 Shell                                    —    □    ×
File  Edit  Shell  Debug  Options  Window  Help
Python 3.7.6 (tags/v3.7.6:43364a7ae0, Dec
19 2019, 00:42:30) [MSC v.1916 64 bit (AM
D64)] on win32
Type "help", "copyright", "credits" or "l
icense()" for more information.
>>> a=10
>>> b=5
>>> print("a+b=",a+b)
a+b= 15
>>> print("a-b=",a-b)
a-b= 5
>>> print("a*b=",a*b)
a*b= 50
>>> print("a/b=",a/b)
a/b= 2.0
>>> print("a%b=",a%b)
a%b= 0
>>> print("a//b=",a//b)
a//b= 2
>>> print("a**b=",a**b)
a**b= 100000
                                              Ln: 19  Col: 4
```

❖ Comparison (Relational) Operators:

- ○ Comparison operators are used to compare values.
- ○ It either returns True or False according to the condition. Assume, a=10 and b=5

Operator	Description	Example
==	If the values of two operands are equal, then the condition become true	(a == b) is not true
!=	If values of two operands are not equal, then condition becomes true.	(a!=b) is true
>	If the value of left operand is greater than the value of right operand, then condition becomes true.	(a > b) is true
<	If the value of left operand is less than the value of right operand, then condition becomes true.	(a < b) is not true.
>=	If the value of left operand is greater than or equal to the value of right operand, then condition becomes true.	(a >= b) is true.
<=	If the value of left operand is less than or equal to the value of right operand, then condition becomes true.	(a <= b) is not true.

```
Python 3.7.6 Shell                              —   □   ×
File  Edit  Shell  Debug  Options  Window  Help
Python 3.7.6 (tags/v3.7.6:43364a7ae0, D
ec 19 2019, 00:42:30) [MSC v.1916 64 bi
t (AMD64)] on win32
Type "help", "copyright", "credits" or
"license()" for more information.
>>> a=10
>>> b=5
>>> print("a>b --->",a>b)
a>b --> True
>>> print("a<b --->",a<b)
a<b --> False
>>> print("a==b --->",a==b)
a==b --> False
>>> print("a!=b --->",a!=b)
a!=b --> True
>>> print("a>=b --->",a>=b)
a>=b --> True
>>> print("a<=b --->",a<=b)
a<=b --> False
                                        Ln: 17   Col: 4
```

❖ **Assignment Operators:**

  ○ Assignment operators are used in Python to assign values to variables.

Operator	Description	Example
=	Assigns values from right side operands to left side operand	c = a + b assigns value of a + b into c
+= Add AND	It adds right operand to the left operand and assign the result to left operand	c += a is equivalent to c = c + a
-=Subtract AND	It subtracts right operand from the left operand and assign the result to left operand	c-=a is equivalent to c = c - a
*= Multiply AND	It multiplies right operand with the left operand and assign the result to left operand	c*=a is equivalent to c = c * a

/= Divide AND	It divides left operand with the right operand and assign the result to left operand	c/=a is equivalent to c = c / a
%=Modulus AND	It takes modulus using two operands and assign the result to left operand	c %= a is equivalent to c = c % a
**= Exponent AND	Performs exponential (power) calculation on operators and assign value to the left operand	c **= a is equivalent to c = c ** a
//=Floor Division	It performs floor division on operators and assign value to the left operand	c //= a is equivalent to c = c // a

```
Python 3.7.6 Shell                                    —    □    ×
File  Edit  Shell  Debug  Options  Window  Help
Type "help", "copyright", "credits" or "license()"
for more information.
>>> a=21
>>> b=10
>>> c=0
>>> c=a+b
>>> print("Line 1 - Value of c is ", c)
Line 1 - Value of c is   31
>>> c += a
>>> print("Line 2 - Value of c is ", c)
Line 2 - Value of c is   52
>>> c *= a
>>> print("Line 3 - Value of c is ", c)
Line 3 - Value of c is   1092
>>> c /= a
>>> print("Line 4 - Value of c is ", c)
Line 4 - Value of c is   52.0
>>> c = 2
>>> c %= a
>>> print("Line 5 - Value of c is ", c)
Line 5 - Value of c is   2
>>> c **= a
>>> print("Line 6 - Value of c is ", c)
Line 6 - Value of c is   2097152
>>> c //= a
>>> print("Line 7 - Value of c is ", c)
Line 7 - Value of c is   99864
                                              Ln: 28  Col: 4
```

❖ **Logical Operators:**

  ○ Logical operators are the and, or, not operators.

Operator	Meaning	Example
and	True if both the operands are true	x and y
or	True if either of the operands is true	x or y
not	True if operand is false (complements the operand)	not x

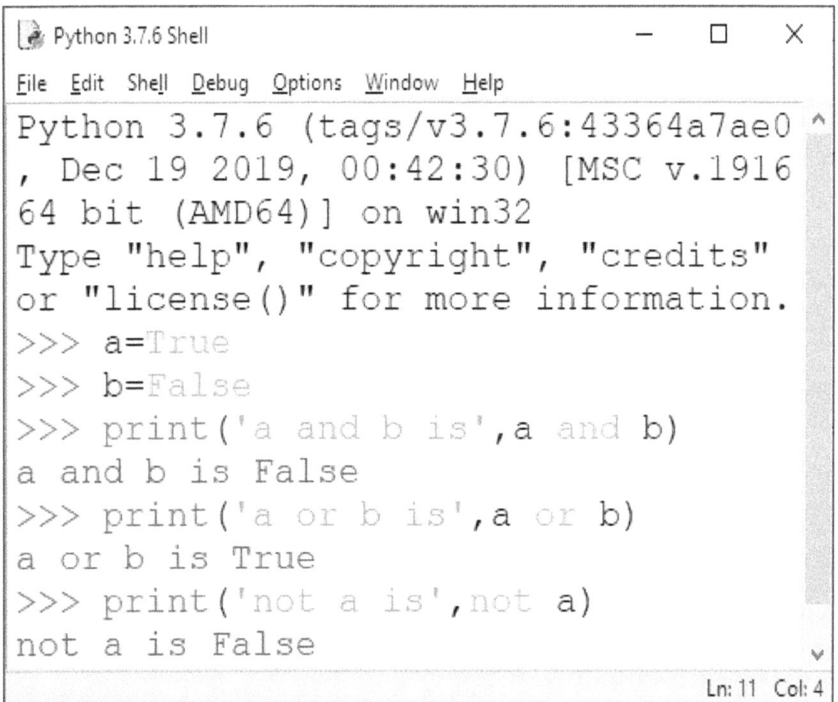

❖ **Bitwise Operators:**

  ○ A bitwise operation operates on one or more-bit patterns
    at the level of individual bits.

Example: Let x = 10 (0000 1010 in binary) and
y = 4 (0000 0100 in binary)

Operator	Meaning	Example
&	Bitwise AND	x& y = 0 (0000 0000)
|	Bitwise OR	x | y = 14 (0000 1110)
~	Bitwise NOT	~x = -11 (1111 0101)
^	Bitwise XOR	x ^ y = 14 (0000 1110)
>>	Bitwise right shift	x>> 2 = 2 (0000 0010)
<<	Bitwise left shift	x<< 2 = 40 (0010 1000)

❖ Membership Operators:

- ○ Evaluates to find a value or a variable is in the specified sequence of string, list, tuple, dictionary or not.
- ○ Let, x=[5,3,6,4,1]. To check particular item in list or not, in and not in operators are used.

Operator	Meaning	Example
in	True if value/variable is found in the sequence	5 in x
not in	True if value/variable is not found in the sequence	5 not in x

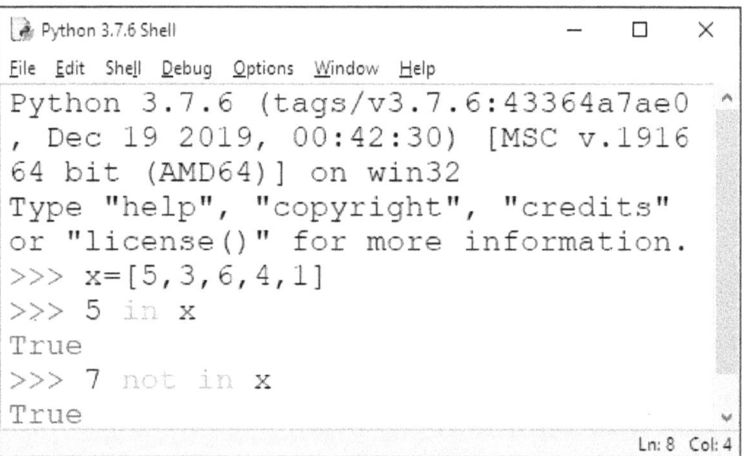

❖ **Identity Operators:**

- o They are used to check if two values (or variables) are located on the same part of the memory.

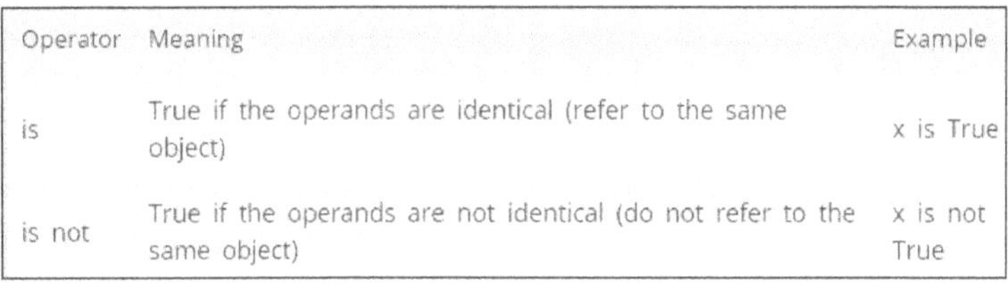

Operator	Meaning	Example
is	True if the operands are identical (refer to the same object)	x is True
is not	True if the operands are not identical (do not refer to the same object)	x is not True

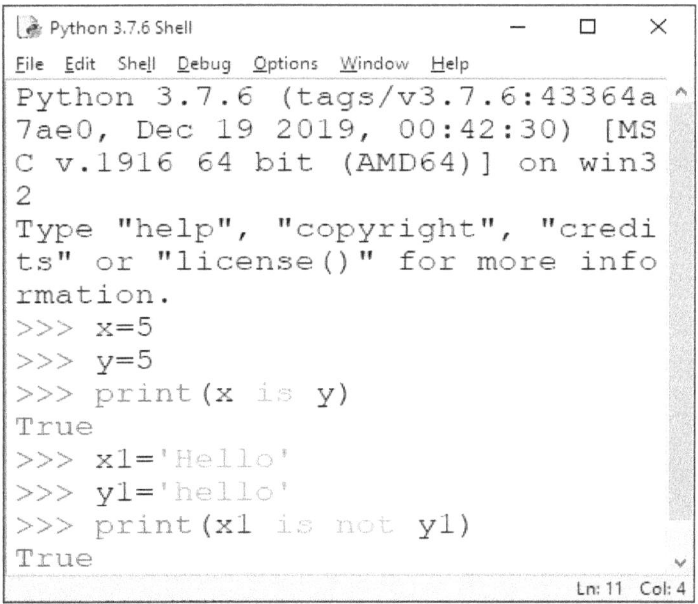

```
Python 3.7.6 (tags/v3.7.6:43364a7ae0, Dec 19 2019, 00:42:30) [MSC v.1916 64 bit (AMD64)] on win32
Type "help", "copyright", "credits" or "license()" for more information.
>>> x=5
>>> y=5
>>> print(x is y)
True
>>> x1='Hello'
>>> y1='hello'
>>> print(x1 is not y1)
True
```

2.9 OPERATOR PRECEDENCE

- o When an expression contains more than one operator, the order of evaluation depends on the order of operations.

Operator Precedence	Description
**	Exponentiation (raise to the power)
~ + -	Complement, unary plus and minus (method names for the last two are +@ and -@)

* / % //	Multiply, divide, modulo and floor division
+ -	Addition and subtraction
>> <<	Right and left bitwise shift
&	Bitwise 'AND'

Operator Precedence	Description
^ |	Bitwise exclusive `OR' and regular `OR'
<= < > >=	Comparison operators
<> == !=	Equality operators
= %= /= //= -= += *= **=	Assignment operators
is is not	Identity operators
in not in	Membership operators
not or and	Logical operators

- o For mathematical operators, Python follows mathematical convention.
- o The acronym PEMDAS (Parentheses, Exponentiation, Multiplication, Division, Addition, Subtraction) is a useful way to remember the rules:
- o Parentheses have the highest precedence and can be used to force an expression to evaluate in the order you want. Since expressions in parentheses are evaluated first, 2 * (3-1) is 4, and (1+1)**(5-2) is 8.
- o You can also use parentheses to make an expression easier to read, as in (minute * 100) / 60, even if it doesn't change the result.
- o Exponentiation has the next highest precedence, so 1 + 2**3 is 9, not 27, and 2*3**2 is 18, not 36.
- o Multiplication and Division have higher precedence than Addition and Subtraction. So, 2*3-1 is 5, not 4, and 6+4/2 is 8, not 5.

- o Operators with the same precedence are evaluated from left to right (except exponentiation).

Example:

a=9-12/3+3*2-1 a=? a=9-4+3*2-1 a=9-4+6-1 a=5+6-1 a=11-1 **a=10**	A=2*3+4%5-3/2+6 A=6+4%5-3/2+6 A=6+4-3/2+6 A=6+4-1+6 A=10-1+6 A=9+6 **A=15**	find m=? m=-43||8&&0||-2 m=-43||0||-2 m=1||-2 **m=1**
a=2,b=12,c=1 d=a<b>c d=2<12>1 d=1>1 **d=0**	a=2,b=12,c=1 d=a<b>c-1 d=2<12>1-1 d=2<12>0 d=1>0 **d=1**	a=2*3+4%5-3//2+6 a=6+4-1+6 a=10-1+6 **a=15**

2.10 FUNCTIONS, FUNCTION DEFINITION AND USE, FUNCTION CALL, FLOW OF EXECUTION, FUNCTION PROTOTYPES, PARAMETERS AND ARGUMENTS, RETURN STATEMENT, ARGUMENTS TYPES, MODULES

2.10.1 Functions

- o Function is a sub program which consists of set of instructions used to perform a specific task. A large program is divided into basic building blocks called function.
- o A function is a block of code which only runs when it is called. You can pass data, known as parameters, into a function. A function can return data as a result.
- o A function is a reusable, ordered piece of code that performs a particular, related action. Functions give your application more modularity and allow you to reuse a lot of code.
- o In Python, a function is a grouping of related statements that performs a calculation, logic, or evaluation operation. The idea is to make a function out of a frequently or repeatedly

performed operation, so that instead of writing the same code over and over for different inputs, we can call the function and reuse the code stored in it. Built-in and user-defined functions are also possible. It aids in keeping the curriculum succinct, non-repetitive, and well-organized.

Need for Function:

➢ When the program is too complex and large, they are divided into parts. Each part is separately coded and combined into single program. Each subprogram is called as function.

➢ Debugging, testing and maintenance becomes easy when the program is divided into subprograms.

➢ Functions are used to avoid rewriting same code again and again in a program.

➢ Function provides code re-usability

➢ The length of the program is reduced.

Types of function:

➢ Functions can be classified into two categories:

- User Defined Function
- Built in function

Built in functions:

○ Built in functions are the functions that are already created and stored in python.

○ These built-in functions are always available for usage and accessed by a programmer. It cannot be modified.

```
Python 3.7.6 Shell
File  Edit  Shell  Debug  Options  Window  Help
>>> max(56,48) #returns maximum value
56
>>> min(67,82) #returns minimum value
67
>>> len('welcome') #returns the length of the given value
7
>>> for i in range(2,8,1):
        print(i)


2
3
4
5
6
7
>>> round(9.6)#returns rounded integer of the given number
10
>>> chr(5)#returns a character (a string) from an integer
'\x05'
>>> float(8) #returns a character (a string) from an integer
8.0
>>> int(5.6)#returns a character (a string) from an integer
5
>>> pow(5,4)#returns power of given number
625
>>> type(8.96)#returns data type of object to which it belongs
<class 'float'>
>>> |
```

User Defined Functions:

- User defined functions are the functions that programmers create for their requirement and use.
- These functions can then be combined to form module which can be used in other programs by importing them.

Advantages of user defined functions:

- Programmers working on large project can divide the workload by making different functions.
- If repeated code occurs in a program, function can be used to include those codes and execute when needed by calling that function.

2.10.2 Function definition: (Sub program)

- def keyword is used to define a function.
- Give the function name after def keyword followed by parentheses in which arguments are given.
- End with colon (:)
- Inside the function add the program statements to be executed
- End with or without return statement

Syntax:

```
def fun_name(Parameter1,Parameter2...Parameter n):
    statement1
    statement2...
    statement n
    return[expression]
```

Example:

```
def my_add(a,b):
    c=a+b
    return c
```

- o Once we have defined a function, we can call it from another function, program or even the Python prompt.
- o To call a function we simply type the function name with appropriate arguments.

Example:

```
x=5
y=4
my_add(x,y)
```

2.10.3 Flow of Execution

- o The order in which statements are executed is called the flow of execution
- o Execution always begins at the first statement of the program.
- o Statements are executed one at a time, in order, from top to bottom.
- o Function definitions do not alter the flow of execution of the program, but remember that statements inside the function are not executed until the function is called.

- o Function calls are like a bypass in the flow of execution. Instead of going to the next statement, the flow jumps to the first line of the called function, executes all the statements there, and then comes back to pick up where it left off.

Note: When you read a program, don't read from top to bottom. Instead, follow the flow of execution. This means that you will read the def statements as you are scanning from top to bottom, but you should skip the statements of the function definition until you reach a point where that function is called.

2.10.4 Function Prototypes

- o Function without arguments and without return type
- o Function with arguments and without return type
- o Function without arguments and with return type
- o Function with arguments and with return type

Function without arguments and without return type

- o In this type no argument is passed through the function call and no output is return to main function
- o The sub function will read the input values perform the operation and print the result in the same block

Function with arguments and without return type

- o Arguments are passed through the function call but output is not return to the main function

Function without arguments and with return type

- o In this type no argument is passed through the function call but output is return to the main function.

Function with arguments and with return type

- o In this type arguments are passed through the function call and output is return to the main function

Without Return Type	
Without argument	**With argument**

def add():
   a=int(input("enter a"))
   b=int(input("enter b"))
   c=a+b
   print(c)
add()
	def add(a,b):
	   c=a+b
	   print(c)
	a=int(input("enter a"))
	b=int(input("enter b"))
	add(a,b)

OUTPUT: enter a 5 enter b 10 15	OUTPUT: enter a 5 enter b 10 15

With return type	
Without argument	**With argument**

def add():
   a=int(input("enter a"))
   b=int(input("enter b"))
   c=a+b
   return c
c=add()
print(c)
	def add(a,b):
	   c=a+b
	   return c
	a=int(input("enter a"))
	b=int(input("enter b"))
	c=add(a,b)
	print(c)

OUTPUT: enter a 5 enter b 10 15	OUTPUT: enter a 5 enter b 10 15

2.10.5 Parameters and Arguments

❖ Parameters:

- Parameters are the value(s) provided in the parenthesis when we write function header. These are the values required by function to work.
- If there is more than one value required, all of them will be listed in parameter list separated by comma.
- Example: def my_add(a,b):

❖ Arguments:

- Arguments are the value(s) provided in function call/ invoke statement.

- o   List of arguments should be supplied in same way as parameters are listed.
- o   Bounding of parameters to arguments is done 1:1, and so there should be same number and type of arguments as mentioned in parameter list.
- o   Example: my_add(x,y)

2.10.6 Return Statement

- o   The return statement is used to exit a function and go back to the place from where it was called.
- o   If the return statement has no arguments, then it will not return any values. But exits from function.

Syntax:

return[expression]

```
Python 3.7.6 Shell                                    —    □    ×
File  Edit  Shell  Debug  Options  Window  Help
Python 3.7.6 (tags/v3.7.6:43364a7ae0
, Dec 19 2019, 00:42:30) [MSC v.1916
64 bit (AMD64)] on win32
Type "help", "copyright", "credits"
or "license()" for more information.
>>> def add(x,y):
        z=x+y
        return z

>>> a=7
>>> b=8
>>> print(add(a,b))
15
                                          Ln: 11  Col: 4
```

2.10.7 Arguments Types

- o   Required Arguments
- o   Keyword Arguments
- o   Default Arguments
- o   Variable length Arguments

Required Arguments:

The number of arguments in the function call should match exactly with the function definition.

```
def my_details( name, age ):
  print("Name: ", name)
  print("Age ", age)
  return
my_details("george",56)
```

Output:

```
Name:  george
Age  56
```

Keyword Arguments:

Python interpreter is able to use the keywords provided to match the values with parameters even though if they are arranged in out of order.

```
def my_details( name, age ):
  print("Name: ", name)
  print("Age ", age)
  return
my_details(age=56,name="george")
```

Output:

```
Name:  george
Age  56
```

Default Arguments:

Assumes a default value if a value is not provided in the function call for that argument.

```
def my_details( name, age=40 ):
   print("Name: ", name)
   print("Age ", age)
   return
my_details(name="george")
```

Output:

```
Name: george
Age  40
```

Variable length Arguments:

If we want to specify more arguments than specified while defining the function, variable length arguments are used. It is denoted by * symbol before parameter.

```
def my_details(*name ):
    print(*name)
my_details("rajan","rahul","micheal",
ärjun")
```

Output:

```
rajan rahul micheal ärjun
```

2.10.8 Modules

- o A module is a file containing Python definitions, functions, statements and instructions.
- o Standard library of Python is extended as modules.
- o To use these modules in a program, programmer needs to import the module.
- o Once we import a module, we can reference or use to any of its functions or variables in our code.

  - There is large number of standard modules also available in python. oStandard modules can be imported the same way as we import our user- defined modules.

- Every module contains many functions.
- To access one of the functions, you have to specify the name of the module and the name of the function separated by dot. This format is called dot notation.

There are **four ways to import a module**

Import: It is simplest and most common way to use modules in our code. Example: import math x=math.pi print("The value of pi is", x) Output: The value of pi is 3.141592653589793	from import : It is used to get a specific function in the code instead of complete file. Example: from math import pi x=pi print("The value of pi is", x) Output: The value of pi is 3.141592653589793
import with renaming: We can import a module by renaming the module as our wish. Example: import math as m x=m.pi print("The value of pi is", x) Output: The value of pi is 3.141592653589793	import all: We can import all names(definitions) form a module using * Example: from math import * x=pi print("The value of pi is", x) Output: The value of pi is 3.141592653589793

Built-in python modules:

- ❖ cmath
- ❖ cytpe
- ❖ html
- ❖ http
- ❖ math
- ❖ map
- ❖ os
- ❖ parser
- ❖ pip
- ❖ sys

ILLUSTRATIVE PROGRAMS

PROGRAM FOR SWAPPING OF VALUES

```
a = int(input("Enter value for a:"))
b = int(input("Enter value for b:"))
c = a
a = b
b = c
print("a=",a,"b=",b)
```

```
Python 3.7.6 (tags/v3.7.6:43364a7ae0, Dec 19 2019, 00:42:30) [MSC v.1916 64 bit (
AMD64)] on win32
Type "help", "copyright", "credits" or "license()" for more information.
>>>
================== RESTART: C:/Program Files/PYTHON/illus1.py ==================
Enter value for a:78
Enter value for b:89
a= 89 b= 78
```

DISTANCE BETWEEN TWO POINTS

```
import math
x1=int(input("enter x1"))
y1=int(input("enter y1"))
x2=int(input("enter x2"))
y2=int(input("enter y2"))
distance =math.sqrt(((x2-x1)**2)+((y2-y1)**2))
print(distance)
```

```
Python 3.7.6 Shell
File Edit Shell Debug Options Window Help
>>>
=================== RESTART: C:/Program Files/PYTHON/illus2.py ==================
enter x1 6
enter y1 14
enter x2 10
enter y2 17
5.0
>>> |
Ln: 34 Col: 4
```

PRGORAM TO CIRCULATE N NUMBERS:

```
illus3.py - C:/Program Files/PYTHON/illus3.py (3.7.6)
File Edit Format Run Options Window Help
a=list(input("enter the list"))
print(a)
for i in range(1,len(a),1):
    print(a[i:]+a[:i])
Ln: 4 Col: 4
```

```
Python 3.7.6 Shell
File Edit Shell Debug Options Window Help
Python 3.7.6 (tags/v3.7.6:43364a7ae0, Dec 19 2019, 00:42:30) [MSC v.1916 64 bit
(AMD64)] on win32
Type "help", "copyright", "credits" or "license()" for more information.
>>>
================== RESTART: C:/Program Files/PYTHON/illus3.py ==================
enter the list1234
['1', '2', '3', '4']
['2', '3', '4', '1']
['3', '4', '1', '2']
['4', '1', '2', '3']
Ln: 10 Col: 4
```

CHAPTER 3

CONTROL STATEMENTS AND FUNCTIONS

> Conditionals: Boolean values, conditional (if), alternative (if-else), chained conditional (if-elif-else); Iteration: state, while, for, break, continue, pass; Fruitful functions: return values, parameters, scope: local and global, composition, recursion; Strings: string slices, immutability, string functions and methods, string module; Lists as arrays. Illustrative programs: square root, gcd, exponentiation, sum the array of numbers, linear search, binary search.

Control statements in python are used to control the order of execution of the program based on the values and logic.

The two main types of control statements are:

- ➢ Conditional Statements
- ➢ Looping or Iterative Statements

3.1 CONDITIONALS

3.1.1 Boolean Values

- ○ Boolean data type has two values. They are 0 and 1.
- ○ 0 represents False
- ○ 1 represents True
- ○ True and False are keyword.

3.1.2 Types of Conditional Statements

- ○ Conditional if

- o   Alternative if... else
- o   Chained if...elif...else
- o   Nested if....else

3.1.2.1 *Conditional if*

Conditional (if) is used to test a condition, if the condition is true the statements inside if will be executed.

Syntax:

```
if(condition 1):
     Statement 1
```

Flowchart:

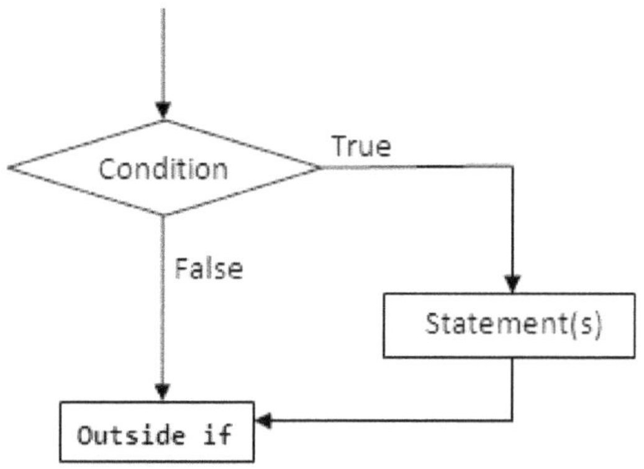

Example:

Program to provide flat rs 500, if the purchase amount is greater than 2000.

```
purchase=int(input("enter your purchase amount"))
if(purchase>=2000):
    purchase=purchase-500
print("amount to pay",purchase)
```

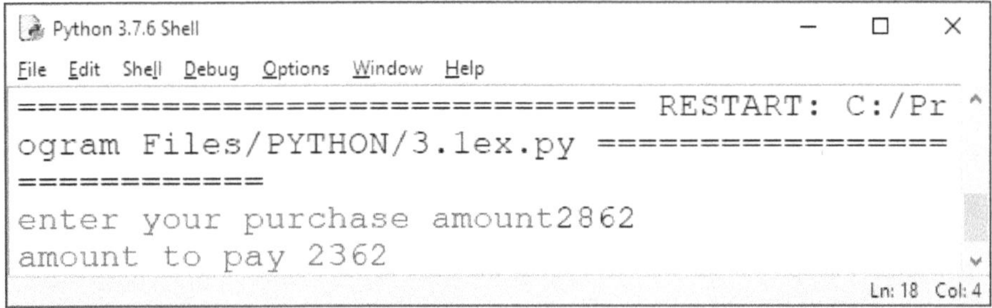

3.1.2.2 Alternative (if-else)

In the alternative the condition must be true or false. In this else statement can be combined with if statement. The else statement contains the block of code that executes when the condition is false. If the condition is true statements inside the if get executed otherwise else part gets executed. The alternatives are called branches, because they are branches in the flow of execution.

syntax:

```
if(condition 1):
    Statement 1
else:
    Statement 2
```

Flowchart:

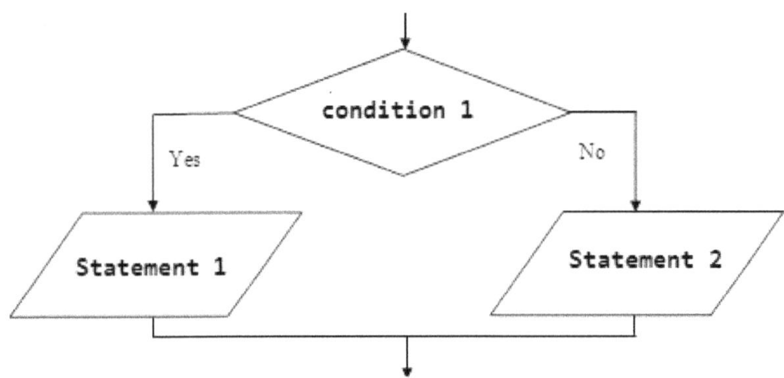

Odd or even number	Output

n=eval(input("enter a number"))
if(n%2==0):
  print("even number")
else:
  print("odd number")
	enter a number4
	even number

positive or negative number	**Output**

n=eval(input("enter a number"))
if(n>=0):
  print("positive number")
else:
  print("negative number")
	enter a number8
	positive number

greatest of two numbers	Output

a=eval(input("enter a value:"))
b=eval(input("enter b value:"))
if(a>b):
  print("greatest:",a)
else:
  print("greatest:",b)
	enter a value:4
	enter b value:7
	greatest: 7

eligibility for voting	**Output**

age=eval(input("enter ur age:"))
if(age>=18):
  print("you are eligible for vote")
else:
  print("you are eligible for vote")
	enter ur age:78
	you are eligible for vote

3.1.2.3 Chained conditionals (if-elif-else)

- ❖ The elif is short for else if.
- ❖ This is used to check more than one condition.
- ❖ If the condition1 is False, it checks the condition2 of the elif block. If all the conditions are False, then the else part is executed.
- ❖ Among the several if...elif...else part, only one part is executed according to the condition.
- ❖ The if block can have only one else block. But it can have multiple elif blocks.
- ❖ The way to express computation like that is a chained conditional.

Syntax:

```
if(condition 1):
    statement 1
elif(condition 2):
    statement 2
elif(condition 3):
    statement 3
else:
    default statement
```

Flowchart:

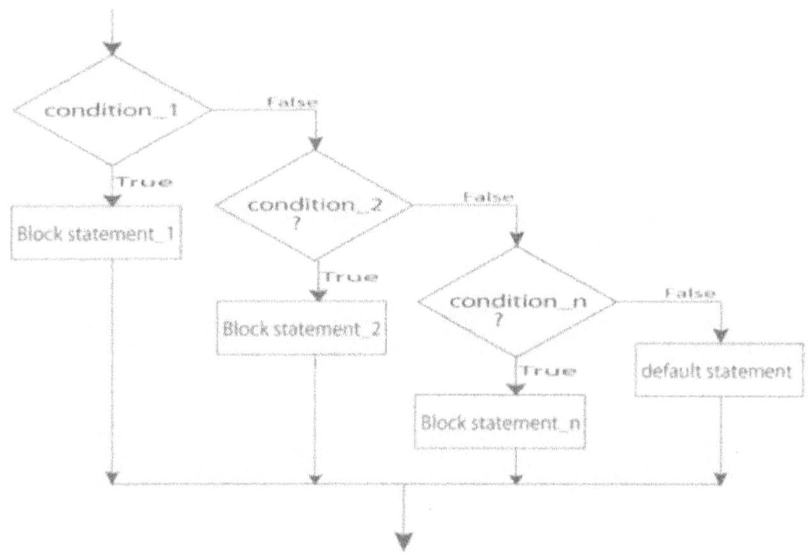

Examples:

- ❖ Student Mark System
- ❖ Traffic Light System
- ❖ Compare 2 Numbers
- ❖ Roots of Quadratic Equation

student mark system	Output

mark=eval(input("enter ur mark:"))
if(mark>=90):
   print("grade:S")
elif(mark>=80):
   print("grade:A")
elif(mark>=70):
   print("grade:B")
elif(mark>=50):
   print("grade:C")
else:
   print("fail")
	enter ur mark:78
	grade:B

traffic light system	**Output**

colour=input("enter colour of light:")
if(colour=="green"):
   print("GO")
elif(colour=="yellow"):
   print("GET READY")
else:
   print("STOP")
	enter colour of light:green
	GO

compare two numbers	Output

x=eval(input("enter x value:"))
y=eval(input("enter y value:"))
if(x == y):
   print("x and y are equal")
elif(x < y):
   print("x is less than y")
else:
   print("x is greater than y")
	enter x value:5
	enter y value:7
	x is less than y

Roots of quadratic equation	**output**

a=eval(input("enter a value:"))
b=eval(input("enter b value:"))
c=eval(input("enter c value:"))
d=(b*b-4*a*c)
if(d==0):
   print("same and real roots")
elif(d>0):
   print("diffrent real roots")
else:
   print("imaginagry roots")
	enter a value:1
	enter b value:0
	enter c value:0
	same and real roots

3.1.2.4 Nested Conditionals

One conditional can also be nested within another. Any number of conditions can be nested inside one another. In this, if the condition is true, it checks another if condition1. If both the conditions are true statement1 get executed otherwise statement2 get execute. If the condition is false statement3 gets executed.

Syntax:

```
if (condition):
      if(condition 1):
          statement 1
      else:
          statement 2
else:
        statement 3
```

Flowchart:

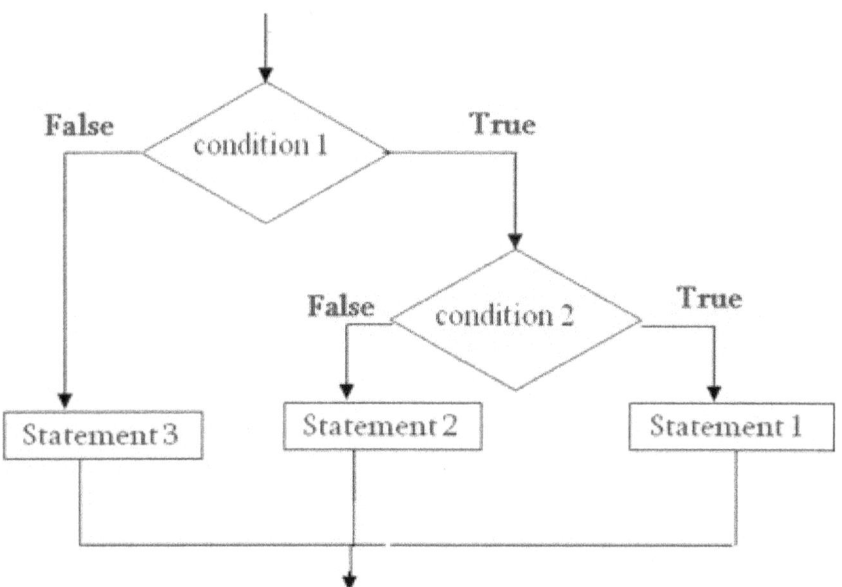

Example:

GREATEST OF 3 NUMBERS

```
a=int(input("enter the value of a"))
b=int(input("enter the value of b"))
c=int(input("enter the value of c"))
if(a>b):
    if(a>c):
        print("The greatest no is",a)
    else:
        print("The greatest no is",c)
else:
    if(b>c):
        print("The greatest no is",b)
    else:
        print("The greatest no is",c)
```

```
Python 3.7.6 (tags/v3.7.6:43364a7ae0, Dec
19 2019, 00:42:30) [MSC v.1916 64 bit (AMD
64)] on win32
Type "help", "copyright", "credits" or "li
cense()" for more information.
>>>
=================== RESTART: C:/Program Fi
les/PYTHON/3.2ex.py ===================
enter the value of a50
enter the value of b43
enter the value of c62
The greatest no is 62
>>>
```

3.2 ITERATIONS/LOPPING STATEMENTS

Types of looping statements are:

- ❖ While Loop
- ❖ For Loop
- ❖ State
- ❖ Break
- ❖ Continue
- ❖ Pass

3.2.1 While Loop

- ❖ While loop statement in Python is used to repeatedly executes set of statement as long as a given condition is true.
- ❖ In while loop, test expression is checked first. The body of the loop is entered only if the test_expression is True. After one iteration, the test expression is checked again. This process continues until the test_expression evaluates to False.
- ❖ In Python, the body of the while loop is determined through indentation.
- ❖ The statements inside the while starts with indentation and the first unintended line marks the end.

Syntax:

```
inital value
while(condition):
    body of while loop
    increment
```

Flowchart:

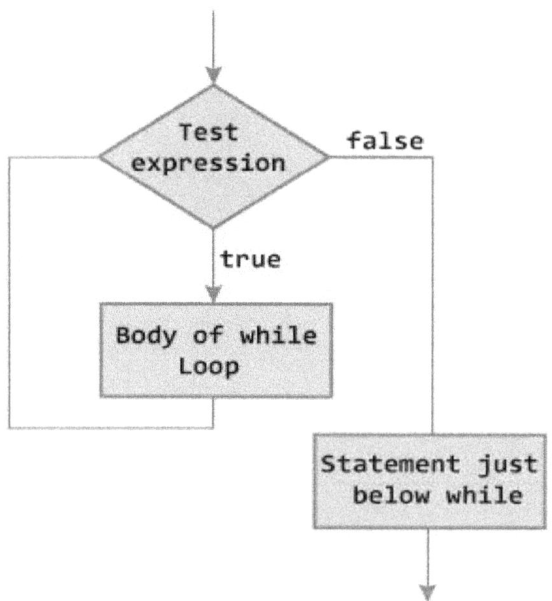

Examples:

1. Program to Find Sum of n Numbers:
2. Program to Find Factorial of a Number
3. Program to Find Sum of Digits of a Number:
4. Program to Reverse the Given Number:
5. Program to Find Number is Armstrong Number or Not
6. Program to Check the Number is Palindrome or Not

SUM of N Numbers

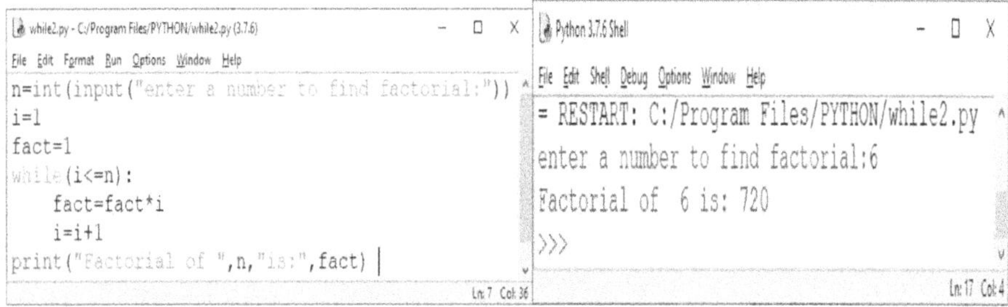

Factorial of a Number

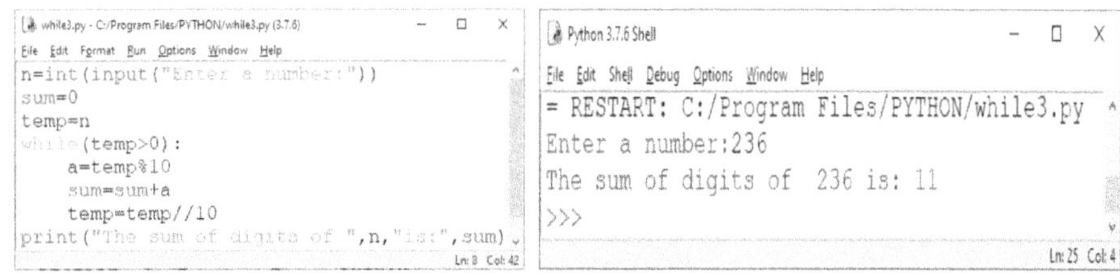

Sum of Digits of a Number:

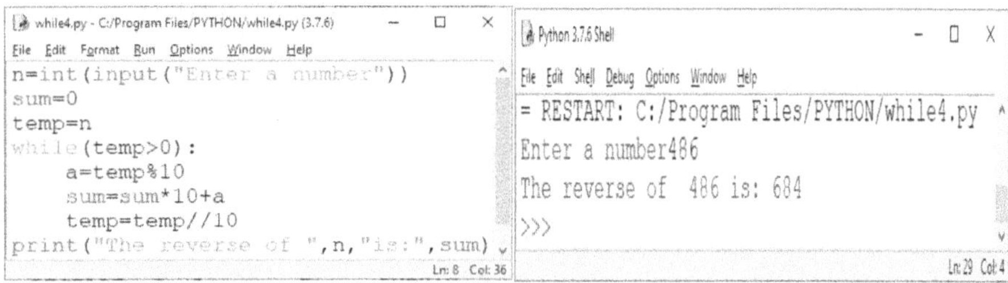

Reverse the given Number:

Armstrong Number

```
n=int(input("Enter a number:"))
org=n
sum=0
while(n>0):
    a=n%10
    sum=sum+a*a*a
    n=n//10
if(sum==org):
    print("The given number is an Armstrong number")
else:
    print("The given number is not an Armstrong number")
```

```
= RESTART: C:/Program Files/PYTHON/while5.py
Enter a number:153
The given number is an Armstrong number
>>>
```

Number Palindrome:

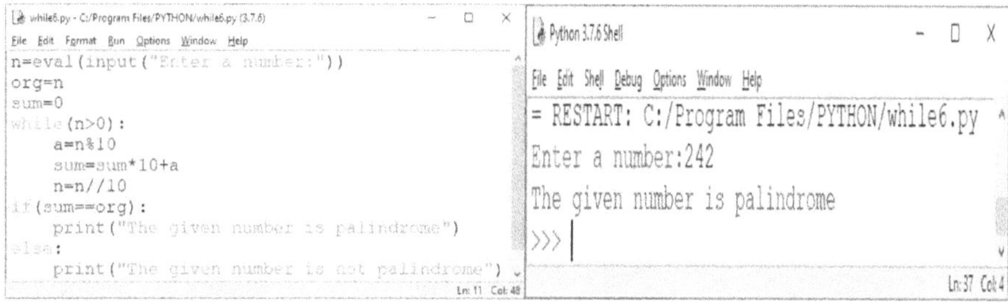

3.2.2 For Loop

for in range:

- ❖ We can generate a sequence using range() function.
- ❖ In range function have to define the start, stop and step size as range(start,stop,step size). step size defaults to 1 if not provided.

Syntax

```
for i in range(start,stop,steps):
     body of for loop
```

Flowchart:

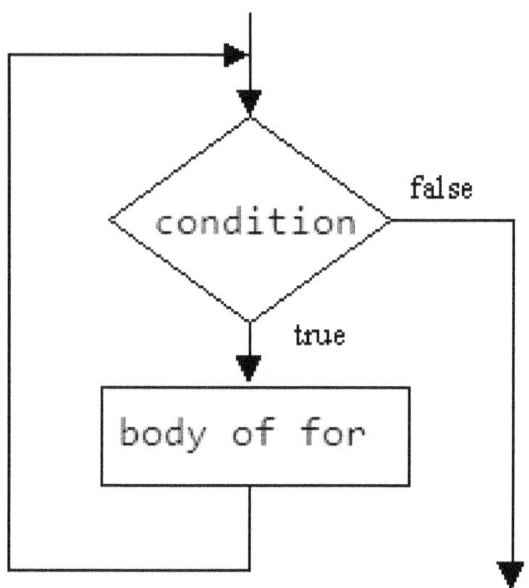

For in sequence

- ❖ The for loop in Python is used to iterate over a sequence (list, tuple, string). Iterating over a sequence is called traversal. Loop continues until we reach the last element in the sequence.
- ❖ The body of for loop is separated from the rest of the code using indentation.

Syntax:

```
for i in sequence:
    print(i)
```

Sequence can be a list, strings or tuples

sequences	example	output
For loop in string	for i in "Ramu": print(i)	R A M U
For loop in list	for i in [2,3,5,6,9]: print(i)	2 3 5 6 9
For loop in tuple	for i in (2,3,1): print(i)	2 3 1

Examples:

1. print nos divisible by 5 not by 10
2. Program to print fibonacci series.
3. Program to find factors of a given number
4. check the given number is perfect number or not
5. check the no is prime or not
6. Print first n prime numbers
7. Program to print prime numbers in range

NUMBER DIVISIBLE BY 5 AND NOT BY 10:

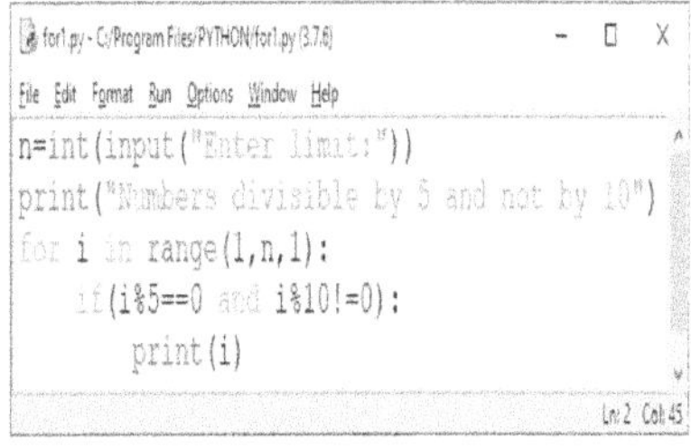

```python
n=int(input("Enter limit:"))
print("Numbers divisible by 5 and not by 10")
for i in range(1,n,1):
    if(i%5==0 and i%10!=0):
        print(i)
```

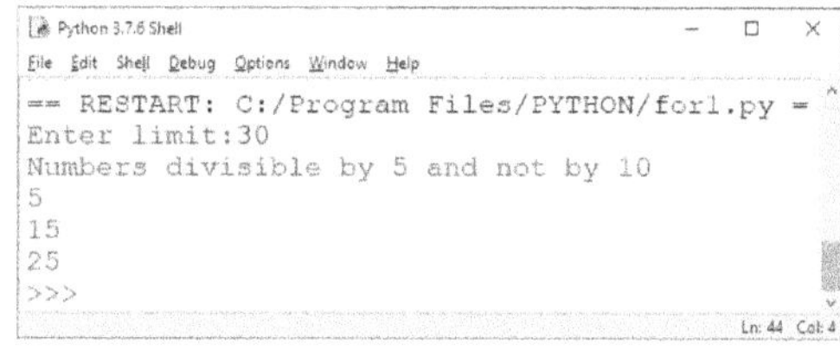

```
== RESTART: C:/Program Files/PYTHON/for1.py =
Enter limit:30
Numbers divisible by 5 and not by 10
5
15
25
>>>
```

FIBONACCI SERIES

```
a=0
b=1
n=eval(input("Enter the number of terms:"))
print("Fibonacci Series:")
print(a,b,end=' ')
for i in range(1,n,1):
    c=a+b
    print(c,end=' ')
    a=b
    b=c
```

```
== RESTART: C:/Program Files/PYTHON/for2.py =
Enter the number of terms:8
Fibonacci Series:
0 1 1 2 3 5 8 13 21
>>>
```

FACTORS OF A GIVEN NUMBER

```
n=int(input("Enter a number:"))
print("The factors are:",end='')
for i in range(1,n+1,1):
    if(n%i==0):
        print(i,end=' ')
```

```
>>>
==== RESTART: C:/Program Files/PYTHON/for3.py ===
Enter a number:48
The factors are:1 2 3 4 6 8 12 16 24 48
>>>
```

PERFECT NUMBER

```
n=eval(input("Enter a number:"))
sum=0
for i in range(1,n,1):
    if(n%i==0):
        sum=sum+i
if(sum==n):
    print("the number is perfect number")
else:
    print("the number is not perfect number")
```

```
>>>
==== RESTART: C:/Program Files/PYTHON/for4.py ===
Enter a number:6
the number is perfect number
>>>
```

PRIME NUMBER

```
n=int(input("Enter a number:"))
if n>1:
    for i in range(2,int(n/2)+1):
        if(n%i)==0:
            print(n,"is not a prime number")
            break
    else:
        print(n,"is a prime number")
else:
    print(n,"is not a prime number")
```

```
>>>
==== RESTART: C:/Program Files/PYTHON/for5.py ===
Enter a number:13
13 is a prime number
>>>
```

FIRST N PRIME NUMBERS

```python
limit=int(input("Enter the limit:"))
print("The first",limit,"prime numbers are:",end=' ')
count=1
n=2
while(count<=limit):
    for i in range(2,n):
        if(n%i==0):
            break
    else:
        print(n,end=' ')
        count=count+1
    n=n+1
```

```
>>>
==== RESTART: C:/Program Files/PYTHON/for6.py ===
Enter the limit:7
The first 7 prime numbers are: 2 3 5 7 11 13 17
>>>
```

PRIME NUMBERS IN A RANGE

```python
lower=int(input("Enter a lower range:"))
upper=int(input("Enter a upper range:"))
print("The prime numbers between",lower,"and",upper,"are:",end=' ')
for n in range(lower,upper + 1):
    if n > 1:
        for i in range(2,n):
            if (n % i) == 0:
                break
        else:
            print(n,end=' ')
```

```
==== RESTART: C:/Program Files/PYTHON/for7.py ===
Enter a lower range:25
Enter a upper range:60
The prime numbers between 25 and 60 are: 29 31 37 41 43 47 53 59
>>>
```

3.2.3 Loop Control Structures:

3.2.3.1 State

Transition from one process to another process under specified condition with in a time is called state.

3.2.3.2 Break

- ❖ Break statements can alter the flow of a loop.
- ❖ It terminates the current
- ❖ loop and executes the remaining statement outside the loop.
- ❖ If the loop has else statement, that will also get terminated and come out of the loop completely.

Syntax:

break

Flowchart

```
while (test Expression):

    // codes
    if (condition for break):

        break

    // codes
```

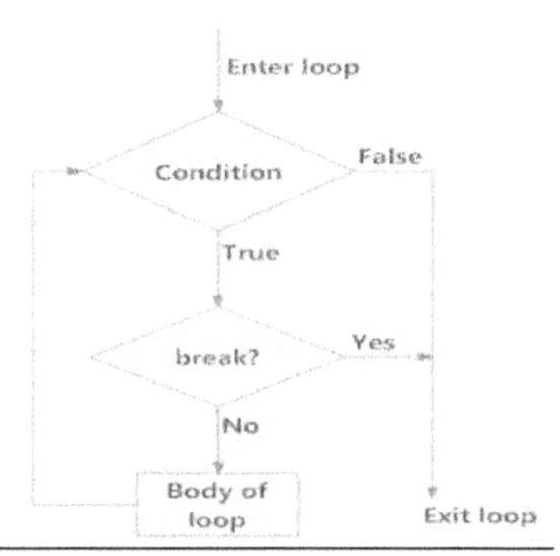

Example

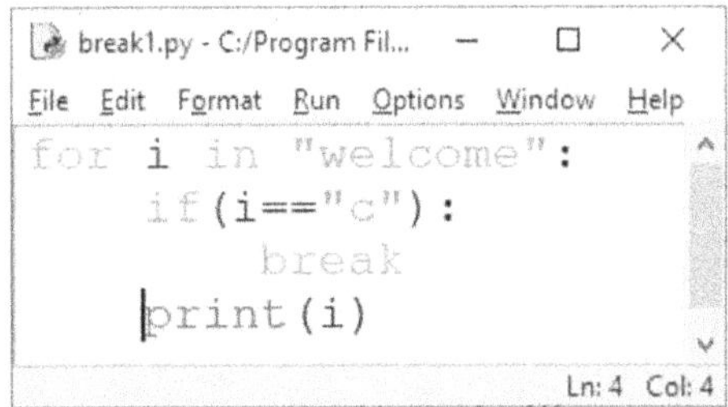

3.2.3.3 Continue

It terminates the current iteration and transfer the control to the next iteration in the loop.

Syntax: Continue

Flowchart

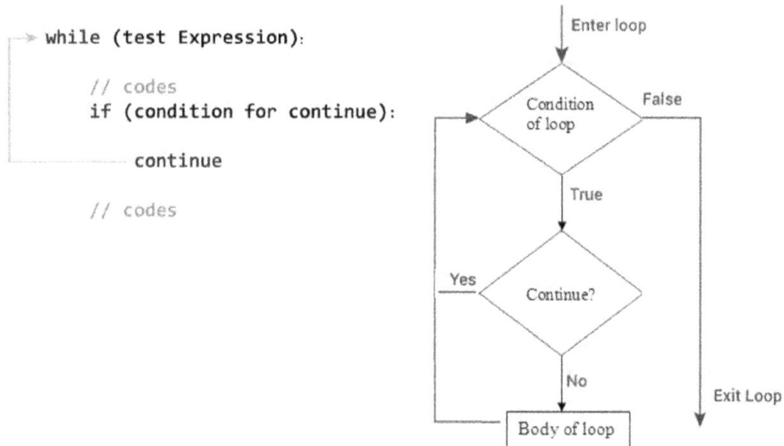

Example

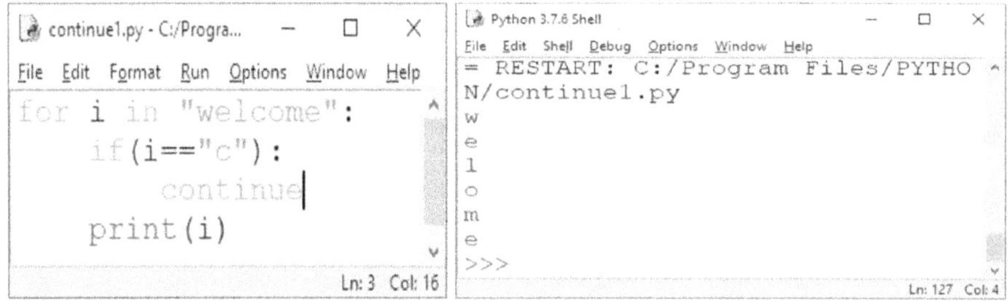

3.2.3.4 Pass

- ❖ It is used when a statement is required syntactically but you don't want any code to execute.
- ❖ It is a null statement; nothing happens when it is executed.

Syntax:

pass

Difference between break and continue

break	continue
It terminates the current loop and executes the remaining statement outside the loop.	It terminates the current iteration and transfer the control to the next iteration in the loop.

3.3 FRUITFUL FUNCTION

A function that returns a value is called fruitful function.

Example 1:

>>> import math

>>> print(math.sqrt(25))

5.0

Example 2:

```
def add():
        a=10
        b=20
        c=a+b
        return c
```

c=add()

print(c)

30

3.3.1 Void Function

A function that performs action but don't return any value.

Example:

print("Hello")

'Helllo'

Example:

```
def add():
        a=10
        b=20
        c=a+b
        print(c)
add()
30
```

3.3.2 Return values

return keywords are used to return the values from the function.

Example:

- ❖ return a – return 1 variable
- ❖ return a,b– return 2 variables
- ❖ return a,b,c– return 3 variables
- ❖ return a+b– return expression
- ❖ return 8– return value

Parameters/Arguments:

❖ Parameters are the variables which used in the function definition. Parameters are inputs to functions. Parameter receives the input from the function call.

❖ It is possible to define more than one parameter in the function definition.

Types of parameters/Arguments:

1. Required/Positional parameters
2. Keyword parameters
3. Default parameters
4. Variable length parameters

Required/ Positional Parameter:

The number of parameters in the function definition should match exactly with number of arguments in the function call.

Example	Output:
def student(name, roll): print(name,roll) student("George",98)	George 98

Keyword parameter:

When we call a function with some values, these values get assigned to the parameter according to their position. When we call functions in keyword parameter, the order of the arguments can be changed.

Example	Output:
def student(name,roll,mark): print(name,roll,mark) student(90,102,"bala")	90 102 bala

Default parameter:

Python allows function parameter to have default values; if the function is called without the argument, the argument gets its default value in function definition.

Variable length parameter

Example	Output:
def student(name, age=17): print (name, age) student("kumar"): student("ajay"):	Kumar 17 Ajay 17

* ❖ Sometimes, we do not know in advance the number of arguments that will be passed into a function.
* ❖ Python allows us to handle this kind of situation through function calls with number of arguments.
* ❖ In the function definition we use an asterisk (*) before the parameter name to denote this is variable length of parameter.

Example	Output:
def student(name,*mark): print(name,mark) student ("bala",102,90)	bala (102 ,90)

3.3.4 Local and Global Scope

Local Scope	Global Scope
A variable with local scope can be used only within the function .	The scope of a variable refers to the places that you can see or access a variable. A variable with global scope can be used anywhere in the program. It can be created by defining a variable outside the function

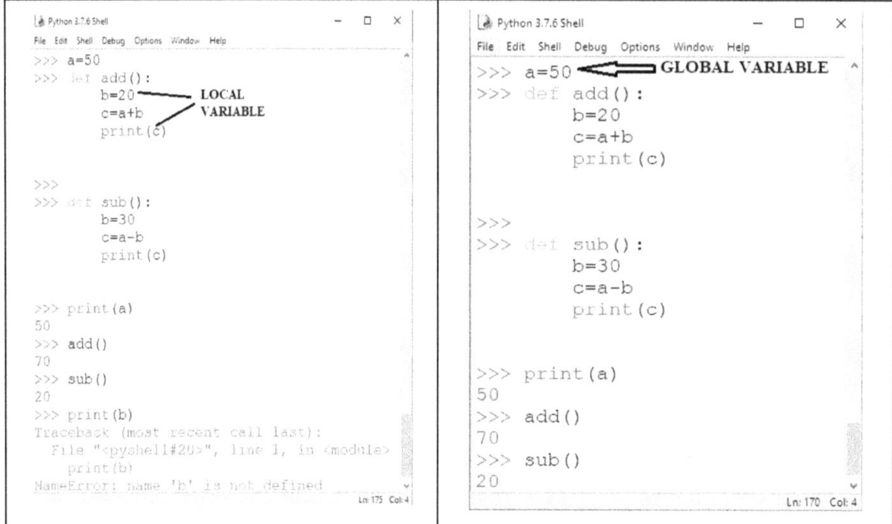

3.3.5 Function Composition

Function Composition is the ability to call one function from within another function.

It is a way of combining functions such that the result of each function is passed as the argument of the next function.

In other words, the output of one function is given as the input of another function is known as function composition.

Example:

Find sum and average using function composition

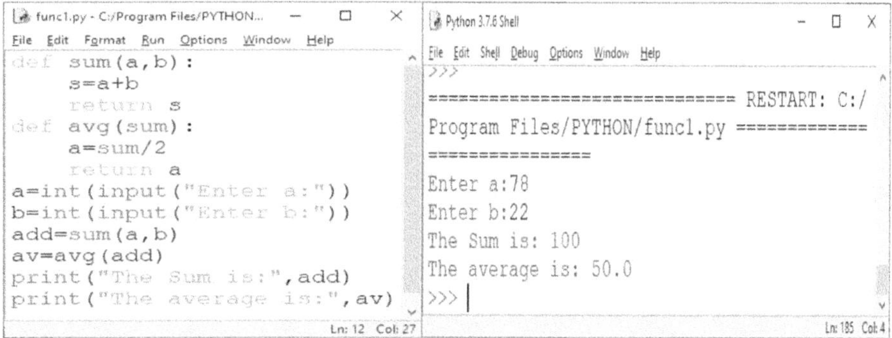

3.3.6 Recursion

A function calling itself till it reaches the base value - stop point of function call.

Example:

Factorial of a given number using recursion

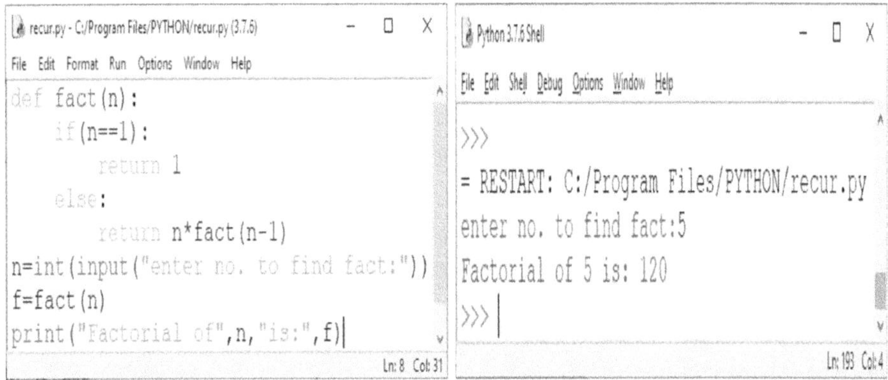

Explanation:

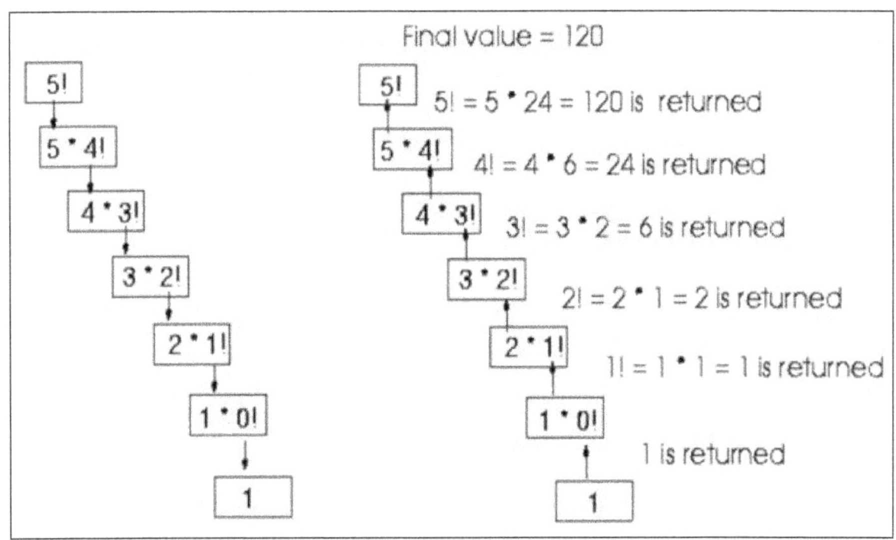

3.4 STRINGS

- ❖ String is defined as sequence of characters represented in quotation marks (either single quotes (') or double quotes (") or triple quotes (""" """).
- ❖ An individual character in a string is accessed using a index.
- ❖ The index should always be an integer (positive or negative).
- ❖ A index starts from 0 to n-1.
- ❖ Strings are immutable i.e. the contents of the string cannot be changed after it is created.
- ❖ Python will get the input at run time by default as a string.
- ❖ Python does not support character data type. A string of size 1 can be treated as characters.

3.4.1 Operations on Strings

1. Indexing
2. Slicing
3. Concatenation
4. Repetitions
5. Membership

String A	H	E	L	L	O
Positive Index	0	1	2	3	4
Negative Index	-5	-4	-3	-2	-1

indexing	```>>>a="HELLO"```
	```>>>print(a[0])```
	```>>>H```
	```>>>print(a[-1])```
	```>>>O```
		❖ Positive indexing helps in accessing the string from the beginning
		❖ Negative subscript helps in accessing the string from the end.

Slicing:	Print[0:4] – HELL Print[:3] – HEL Print[0:]- HELLO	The Slice[start : stop] operator extracts sub string from the strings. A segment of a string is called a slice.
Concatenation	a="save" b="earth" >>>print(a+b) saveearth	The + operator joins the text on both sides of the operator.
Repetitions:	a="panimalar " >>>print(3*a) panimalarpanimalar panimalar	The * operator repeats the string on the left hand side times the value on right hand side.

Membership:	>>> s="good morning"
	>>>"m" in s
	True
	>>> "a" not in s
	True
		Using membership operators to check a particular character is in string or not.
		Returns true if present

3.4.3 String Slices

❖ A part of a string is called string slices.
❖ The process of extracting a sub string from a string is called slicing.

Slicing: a="HELLO"	Print[0:4] – HELL Print[:3] – HEL Print[0:]- HELLO	The Slice[n : m] operator extracts sub string from the strings. A segment of a string is called a slice.

3.4.4 Immutability

❖ Python strings are "immutable" as they cannot be changed after they are created.
❖ Therefore [ ] operator cannot be used on the left side of an assignment.

operations	Example	output
element assignment	a="PYTHON" a[0]='x'	TypeError: 'str' object does not support element assignment
element deletion	a="PYTHON" del a[0]	TypeError: 'str' object doesn't support element deletion
delete a string	a="PYTHON" del a	NameError: name 'my_string' is not defined

3.4.5 String Built-in Methods

a="happy birthday"

Here, a is the string name.

	syntax	example	description
1	a.capitalize()	>>> a.capitalize() ' Happy birthday'	capitalize only the first letter in a string
2	a.upper()	>>> a.upper() 'HAPPY BIRTHDAY'	change string to upper case
3	a.lower()	>>> a.lower() ' happy birthday'	change string to lower case
4	a.title()	>>> a.title() ' Happy Birthday '	change string to title case i.e. first characters of all the words are capitalized.
5	a.swapcase()	>>> a.swapcase() 'HAPPY BIRTHDAY'	change lowercase characters to uppercase and vice versa
6	a.split()	>>> a.split() ['happy', 'birthday']	returns a list of words separated by space
7	a.center(width,"fillchar")	>>>a.center(19,"*") '***happy birthday***'	pads the string with the specified "fillchar" till the length is equal to "width"
8	a.count(substring)	>>> a.count('happy') 1	returns the number of occurences of substring
9	a.replace(old,new)	>>>a.replace('happy', 'wishyou happy') 'wishyou happy birthday'	replace all old substrings with new substrings

10	a.join(b)	>>> b="happy"
		>>> a="-"
		>>> a.join(b)
		'h-a-p-p-y'
			returns a string concatenated with the elements of an iterable. (Here "a" is the iterable)

11	a.isupper()	>>> a.isupper() False	checks whether all the case-based characters (letters) of the string are uppercase.
12	a.islower()	>>> a.islower() True	checks whether all the case-based characters (letters) of the string are lowercase.
13	a.isalpha()	>>> a.isalpha() False	checks whether the string consists of alphabetic characters only.

	syntax	example	description
14	a.isalnum()	>>> a.isalnum() False	checks whether the string consists of alphanumeric characters.
15	a.isdigit()	>>> a.isdigit() False	checks whether the string consists of digits only.
16	a.isspace()	>>> a.isspace() False	checks whether the string consists of whitespace only.
17	a.istitle()	>>> a.istitle() False	checks whether string is title cased.
18	a.startswith(substring)	>>> a.startswith("h") True	checks whether string starts with substring
19	a.endswith(substring)	>>> a.endswith("y") True	checks whether the string ends with the substring
20	a.find(substring)	>>> a.find("happy") 0	returns index of substring, if it is found. Otherwise -1 is returned.
21	len(a)	>>>len(a) >>>14	Return the length of the string
22	min(a)	>>>min(a) >>>' '	Return the minimum character in the string
23	max(a)	max(a) >>>'y'	Return the maximum character in the string

3.4.6 String Modules

❖ A module is a file containing Python definitions, functions, statements.

❖ Standard library of Python is extended as modules.

❖ To use these modules in a program, programmer needs to import the module.

❖ Once we import a module, we can reference or use to any of its functions or variables in our code.

❖ There is large number of standard modules also available in python.

❖ Standard modules can be imported the same way as we import our user-defined modules.

Syntax:

import module_name

Example	output
import string print(string.punctuation) print(string.digits) print(string.printable) print(string.capwords("happy birthday")) print(string.hexdigits) print(string.octdigits)	!"#$%&'()*+,-./:;<=>?@[\]^_`{\|}~ 0123456789 0123456789abcdefghijklmnopqrstuvwxyzABCDEFGHIJ KLMNOPQRSTUVWXYZ!"#$%&'()*+,- ./:;<=>?@[\]^_`{|}~ Happy Birthday 0123456789abcdefABCDEF 01234567

3.4.7 Escape Sequence in String

Escape Sequence	Description	example
\n	new line	>>> print("hai \nhello") hai hello
\\	prints Backslash (\)	>>> print("hai\\hello") hai\hello
\'	prints Single quote (')	>>> print("'") '
\"	prints Double quote (")	>>>print("\"") "
\t	prints tab sapace	>>>print("hai\thello") hai hello
\a	ASCII Bell (BEL)	>>>print("\a")

3.5 LIST AS ARRAYS

Array:

Array is a collection of similar elements. Elements in the array can be accessed by index. Index starts with 0. Array can be handled in python by module named array. To create array, have to import array module in the program.

Syntax:

import array

Syntax to create array:

Array_name = module_name.function_name('datatype',[elements])

Example:

a=array.array('i',[1,2,3,4])

a- array name

array- module name i- integer datatype

Program to find sum of array elements

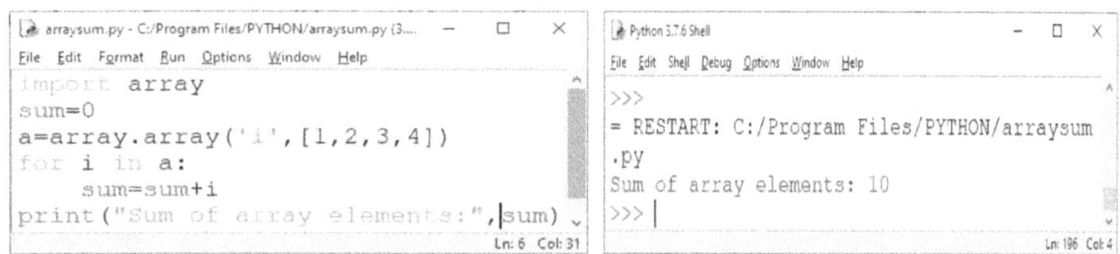

3.5.1 Convert List into array

fromlist() function is used to append list to array. Here the list is act like a array.

Syntax:

arrayname.fromlist(list_name)

Example

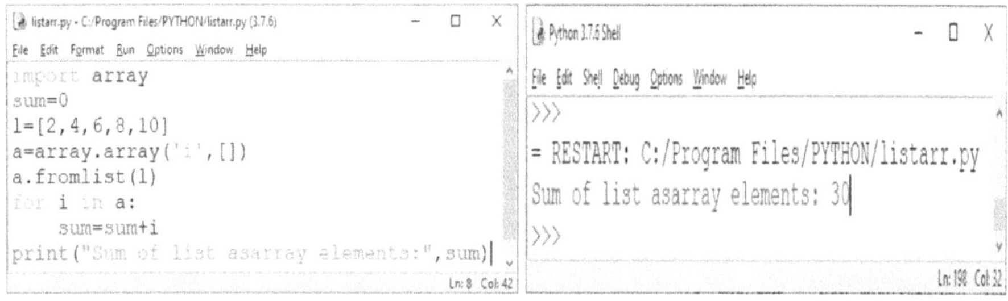

3.5.2 Methods in Array

Given an list a=[1,2,3,4,5], the following table show built-in methods used for array:

Syntax	example	Description
array(data type, value list)	array('i',[2,3,4,5])	This function is used to create an array with data type and value list specified in its arguments.
append()	>>>a.append(6) [2,3,4,5,6]	This method is used to add the at the end of the array.
insert(index,element)	>>>a.insert(2,10) [2,3,10,5,6]	This method is used to add the value at the position specified in its argument.
pop(index)	>>>a.pop(1) [2,10,5,6]	This function removes the element at the position mentioned in its argument, and returns it.
index(element)	>>>a.index(2) 0	This function returns the index of value
reverse()	>>>a.reverse() [6,5,10,2]	This function reverses the array.
count()	a.count() 4	This is used to count number of elements in array

3.6 ILLUSTRATIVE PROGRAMS

Square Root using Newton's Methods

```
newtonsqrt.py - C:/Program Files/PYTHON/newtonsqrt.py (3.7.6)      —   □   ×
File  Edit  Format  Run  Options  Window  Help
def newtonsqrt(n):
    root=n/2
    for i in range(10):
        root=(root+n/root)/2
    print("The square root of",n,"is:",root)
n=eval(input("Enter number to find Sqrt:"))
newtonsqrt(n)
                                                          Ln: 7  Col: 13
```

```
Python 3.7.6 Shell                                        —    □    ×
File  Edit  Shell  Debug  Options  Window  Help
= RESTART: C:/Program Files/PYTHON/newtonsqrt
.py
Enter number to find Sqrt:64
The square root of 64 is: 8.0
                                                        Ln: 203  Col: 0
```

GCD of 2 numbers

```
GCD.py - C:\Program Files\PYTHON\GCD.py (3.7.6)           —    □    ×
File  Edit  Format  Run  Options  Window  Help
print("========GCD OF TWO NUMBERS=========")
n1=int(input("enter a number:"))
n2=int(input("enter another number:"))
rem=n1%n2
while rem!=0:
    n1=n2
    n2=rem
    rem=n1%n2
print("GCD of given numbers is:",n2)
                                                        Ln: 9  Col: 36
```

```
Python 3.7.6 Shell                                        —    □    ×
File  Edit  Shell  Debug  Options  Window  Help
== RESTART: C:\Program Files\PYTHON\GCD.py ==
========GCD OF TWO NUMBERS========
enter a number:36
enter another number:18
GCD of given numbers is: 18
>>>
                                                        Ln: 209  Col: 4
```

Exponent of a Number:

```
exp.py - C:\Program Files\PYTHON\exp.py (3.7.6)           —    □    ×
File  Edit  Format  Run  Options  Window  Help
print("====exponentiation of a number====")
n=int(input("Enter number:"))
e=int(input("Enter exponent:"))
r=n
for i in range(1,e):
    r=n*r
print("Exponentiation is:",r)
                                                        Ln: 1  Col: 0
```

```
Python 3.7.6 Shell                                    —    □    ×
File  Edit  Shell  Debug  Options  Window  Help
== RESTART: C:\Program Files\PYTHON\exp.py ==
====exponentiation of a number====
Enter number:3
Enter exponent:3
Exponentiation is: 27
>>> |
                                            Ln: 215  Col: 4
```

Linear Search

```
LS.py - C:\Program Files\PYTHON\LS.py (3.7.6)          —    □    ×
File  Edit  Format  Run  Options  Window  Help
alist= [4, 2, 8, 9, 3, 7]
print("List is:",alist)
print("=========LINEAR SEARCH==========")
x = int(input("Enter number to search: "))
found = False
for i in range(len(alist)):
    if(alist[i] == x):
        found = True
        print("%d found at %dth position"%(x,i+1))
        break
if(found == False):
    print("%d is not in list"%x)
                                            Ln: 12  Col: 32
```

```
Python 3.7.6 Shell                                    —    □    ×
File  Edit  Shell  Debug  Options  Window  Help
=== RESTART: C:\Program Files\PYTHON\LS.py ==
List is: [4, 2, 8, 9, 3, 7]
=========LINEAR SEARCH==========
Enter number to search: 9
9 found at 4th position
>>> |
                                            Ln: 221  Col: 4
```

Binary Search

```
def binarySearch(alist, item):
    first = 0
    last = len(alist)-1
    while first<=last:
        midpoint = (first + last)//2
        if (alist[midpoint]==item):
            print(item,"found at position:",midpoint+1)
            break
        elif item <alist[midpoint]:
            last = midpoint-1
        else:
            first = midpoint+1
    else:
        print("The element not found")
print("========BINARY SEARCH========")
blist= [0,1,2,8,13,17,19,32,42]
print("List is:",blist)
search=int(input("Enter the element to be search"))
binarySearch(blist, search)
```

```
=== RESTART: C:\Program Files\PYTHON\BS.py ==
========BINARY SEARCH========
List is: [0, 1, 2, 8, 13, 17, 19, 32, 42]
Enter the element to be search13
13 found at position: 5
>>>
```

CHAPTER 4

COMPOUND DATA: LISTS, TUPLES, DICTIONARIES

> **Lists**, list operations, list slices, list methods, list loop, mutability, aliasing, cloning lists, list parameters; **Tuples**, tuple assignment, tuple as return value; **Dictionaries**: operations and methods; advanced list processing - list comprehension, **Illustrative programs:** selection sort, insertion sort, merge sort, quick sort.

4.1 LISTS

- ❖ List is an ordered sequence of items. Values in the list are called elements / items.
- ❖ It can be written as a list of comma-separated items (values) between **square brackets[ ]**.
- ❖ Items in the lists can be of different data types.

4.1.1 Operations on list

- ❖ Indexing
- ❖ Slicing
- ❖ Concatenation
- ❖ Repetitions
- ❖ Updating
- ❖ Membership
- ❖ Comparison

operations	examples	description

create a list	>>> a=[2,3,4,5,6,7,8,9,10]
	>>> print(a)
	[2, 3, 4, 5, 6, 7, 8, 9, 10]
		in this way we can create a list at compile time

Indexing	>>> print(a[0])
	2
	>>> print(a[8])
	10
	>>> print(a[-1])
	10
		Accessing the item in the position 0
		Accessing the item in the position 8
		Accessing a last element using negative indexing.

Slicing	>>> print(a[0:3])
	[2, 3, 4]
	>>> print(a[0:])
	[2, 3, 4, 5, 6, 7, 8, 9, 10]
		Printing a part of the list.

Concatenation	>>>b=[20,30] >>> print(a+b) [2, 3, 4, 5, 6, 7, 8, 9, 10, 20, 30]	Adding and printing the items of two lists.
Repetition	>>> print(b*3) [20, 30, 20, 30, 20, 30]	Create a multiple copies of the same list.

Updating	>>> print(a[2])
	4
	>>> a[2]=100
	>>> print(a)
	[2, 3, 100, 5, 6, 7, 8, 9, 10]
		Updating the list using index value.

Membership	>>> a=[2,3,4,5,6,7,8,9,10]
	>>> 5 in a
	True
	>>> 100 in a
	False
	>>> 2 not in a
	False
		Returns True if element is present in list. Otherwise returns false.

Comparison	>>> a=[2,3,4,5,6,7,8,9,10]
	>>>b=[2,3,4]
	>>> a==b
	False
	>>> a!=b
	True
		Returns True if all elements in both elements are same. Otherwise returns false

<u>4.1.2 List Slices</u>

List slicing is an operation that extracts a subset of elements from an list and packages them as another list.

Syntax:

Listname[start:stop]

Listname[start:stop:steps]

- ❖ default start value is 0
- ❖ default stop value is n-1
- ❖   [:] this will print the entire list

slices	example	description

a[0:3]	>>> a=[9,8,7,6,5,4]
	>>> a[0:3]
	[9, 8, 7]
		Printing a part of a list from 0 to 2.

a[:4]	>>> a[:4] [9, 8, 7, 6]	Default start value is 0. so prints from 0 to 3
a[1:]	>>> a[1:] [8, 7, 6, 5, 4]	default stop value will be n-1. so prints from 1 to 5
a[:]	>>> a[:] [9, 8, 7, 6, 5, 4]	Prints the entire list.

slices	example	description
a[2:2]	>>> a[2:2] [ ]	print an empty slice
a[0:6:2]	>>> a[0:6:2] [9, 7, 5]	Slicing list values with step size 2.
a[::-1]	>>> a[::-1] [4, 5, 6, 7, 8, 9]	Returns reverse of given list values

4.1.3 List Methods

- ❖ Methods used in lists are used to manipulate the data quickly.
- ❖ These methods work only on lists.
- ❖ They do not work on the other sequence types that are not mutable, that is, the values they contain cannot be changed, added, or deleted.

syntax:

list name.method name(element/index/list)

syntax	example	description

a.append(element)	>>> a=[1,2,3,4,5]
	>>> a.append(6)
	>>> print(a)
	[1, 2, 3, 4, 5, 6]
		Add an element to the end of the list

a.insert(index,element)	>>> a.insert(0,0)
	>>> print(a)
	[0, 1, 2, 3, 4, 5, 6]
		Insert an item at the defined index

a.extend(b)	>>> b=[7,8,9]
	>>> a.extend(b)
	>>> print(a)
	[0, 1, 2, 3, 4, 5, 6, 7, 8,9]
		Add all elements of a list to the another list

a.index(element)	>>> a.index(8) 8	Returns the index of the first matched item

a.sort()	>>> a.sort()
	>>> print(a)
	[0, 1, 2, 3, 4, 5, 6, 7, 8]
		Sort items in a list in ascending order

a.reverse()	>>> a.reverse()
	>>> print(a)
	[8, 7, 6, 5, 4, 3, 2, 1, 0]
		Reverse the order of items in the list

4.1.4 List Loops

a.pop()	>>> a.pop() 0	Removes and returns an element at the last element
a.pop(index)	>>> a.pop(0) 8	Remove the particular element and return it.

a.remove(element)	>>> a.remove(1)
	>>> print(a)
	[7, 6, 5, 4, 3, 2]
		Removes an item from the list

a.count(element)	>>> a.count(6) 1	Returns the count of number of items passed as an argument

a.copy()	>>> b=a.copy()
	>>> print(b)
	[7, 6, 5, 4, 3, 2]
		Returns a shallow copy of the list

len(list)	>>> len(a) 6	return the length of the length
min(list)	>>> min(a) 2	return the minimum element in a list
max(list)	>>> max(a) 7	return the maximum element in a list.

a.clear()	>>> a.clear()
	>>> print(a)
	[ ]
		Removes all items from the list.

del(a)	>>> del(a)
	>>> print(a)
	Error: name 'a' is not defined
		delete the entire list.

4.1.4.1 List using For Loop

- ❖ The for loop in Python is used to iterate over a sequence (list, tuple, string) or other iterable objects.
- ❖ Iterating over a sequence is called traversal.
- ❖ Loop continues until we reach the last item in the sequence.
- ❖ The body of for loop is separated from the rest of the code using indentation.

Accessing element	output
a=[10,20,30,40,50] for i in a: print(i)	1 2 3 4 5

Accessing index	output
a=[10,20,30,40,50] for i in range(0,len(a),1): print(i)	0 1 2 3 4

Accessing element using range:	output
a=[10,20,30,40,50] for i in range(0,len(a),1): print(a[i])	10 20 30 40 50

4.1.4.2 List using While loop

* The while loop in Python is used to iterate over a block of code as long as the test expression (condition) is true.
* When the condition is tested and the result is false, the loop body will be skipped and the first statement after the while loop will be executed.

Sum of elements in list	Output

a=[1,2,3,4,5]
i=0
sum=0
while i<len(a):
    sum=sum+a[i]
    i=i+1
print(sum)
	15

4.1.4.3 Infinite Loop

A loop becomes infinite loop if the condition given never becomes false. It keeps on running. Such loops are called infinite loop.

4.1.5 Mutability

- ❖ Lists are mutable. (can be changed)
- ❖ Mutability is the ability for certain types of data to be changed without entirely recreating it.
- ❖ An item can be changed in a list by accessing it directly as part of the assignment statement.
- ❖ Using the indexing operator (square brackets[ ]) on the left side of an assignment, one of the list items can be updated.

Example	Description

>>> a=[1,2,3,4,5]
>>> a[0]=100
>>> print(a)
[100, 2, 3, 4, 5]
	changing single element

>>> a=[1,2,3,4,5]
>>> a[0:3]=[100,100,100]
>>> print(a)
[100, 100, 100, 4, 5]
	changing multiple element

>>> a=[1,2,3,4,5]
>>> a[0:3]=[ ]
>>> print(a)
[4, 5]
	The elements from a list can also be removed by assigning the empty list to them.

>>> a=[1,2,3,4,5]
>>> a[0:0]=[20,30,45]
>>> print(a)
[20,30,45,1, 2, 3, 4, 5]
	The elements can be inserted into a list by squeezing them into an empty slice at the desired location.

4.1.6 Aliasing

- ❖ Creating a copy of a list is called aliasing. When you create a copy both list will be
- ❖ having same memory location. changes in one list will affect another list.
- ❖ Aliasing refers to having different names for same list values.

Example	Output
a= [1, 2, 3 ,4 ,5] b=a print (b) a is b a[0]=100 print(a) print(b)	 [1, 2, 3, 4, 5] True [100,2,3,4,5] [100,2,3,4,5]

- ❖ In this a single list object is created and modified using the subscript operator.
- ❖ When the first element of the list named "a" is replaced, the first element of the list named "b" is also replaced.
- ❖ This type of change is what is known as a side effect. This happens because after the assignment b=a, the variables a and b refer to the exact same list object.

❖ They are aliases for the same object. This phenomenon is known as aliasing.

❖ To prevent aliasing, a new object can be created and the contents of the original can be copied which is called cloning.

4.1.7 Clonning

❖ To avoid the disadvantages of copying we are using cloning. creating a copy of a

❖ same list of elements with two different memory locations is called cloning.

❖ Changes in one list will not affect locations of aother list.

❖ Cloning is a process of making a copy of the list without modifying the original list.

❖ Methods of clonning:

- Slicing
- list()method
- copy() method

clonning using Slicing
>>>a=[1,2,3,4,5] >>>b=a[:] >>>print(b) [1,2,3,4,5] >>>a is b False
clonning using List( ) method
>>>a=[1,2,3,4,5] >>>b=list >>>print(b) [1,2,3,4,5] >>>a is b false >>>a[0]=100 >>>print(a) >>>a=[100,2,3,4,5] >>>print(b) >>>b=[1,2,3,4,5]
clonning using copy() method

a=[1,2,3,4,5]
>>>b=a.copy()
>>> print(b)
[1, 2, 3, 4, 5]
>>> a is b
False

4.1.8 List as Parameters

- ❖ In python, arguments are passed by reference.
- ❖ If any changes are done in the parameter which refers within the function, then the changes also reflect back in the calling function.
- ❖ When a list to a function is passed, the function gets a reference to the list.
- ❖ Passing a list as an argument actually passes a reference to the list, not a copy of the list.

def remove(a): a.remove(1) a=[1,2,3,4,5] remove(a) print(a)	[2,3,4,5]

def insert(a): a.insert(0,30) a=[1,2,3,4,5] insert(a) print(a)	[30, 1, 2, 3, 4, 5]

4.2 TUPLES

- ❖ Since lists are mutable, changes made to the elements referenced by the parameter change the same list that the argument is referencing.
- ❖ A tuple is same as list, except that the set of elements is enclosed in parentheses
- ❖ instead of square brackets.
- ❖ A tuple is an immutable list. i.e. once a tuple has been created, you can't add elements to a tuple or remove elements from the tuple.

❖ But tuple can be converted into list and list can be converted in to tuple.

methods	example	description

list( )	>>> a=(1,2,3,4,5)
	>>> a=list(a)
	>>> print(a) [1, 2, 3, 4, 5]
		It converts the given tuple into list.

tuple( )	>>> a=[1,2,3,4,5]
	>>> a=tuple(a)
	>>> print(a) (1, 2, 3, 4, 5)
		It converts the given list into tuple.

4.2.1 Benefit of Tuple

❖ Tuples are faster than lists.
❖ If the user wants to protect the data from accidental changes, tuple can be used.
❖ Tuples can be used as keys in dictionaries, while lists can't.

4.2.3 Operations on Tuples

❖ Indexing
❖ Slicing
❖ Concatenation
❖ Repetitions
❖ Membership
❖ Comparison

4.2.4 Tuple Methods

Operations	examples	description
Creating a tuple	>>>a=(20,40,60,"apple","ball")	Creating the tuple with elements of different data types.
Indexing	>>>print(a[0]) 20 >>> a[2] 60	Accessing the item in the position 0 Accessing the item in the position 2
Slicing	>>>print(a[1:3]) (40,60)	Displaying items from 1st till 2nd.
Concatenation	>>> b=(2,4) >>>print(a+b) >>>(20,40,60,"apple","ball",2,4)	Adding tuple elements at the end of another tuple elements
Repetition	>>>print(b*2) >>>(2,4,2,4)	repeating the tuple in n no of times

Membership	>>> a=(2,3,4,5,6,7,8,9,10)
	>>> 5 in a
	True
	>>> 100 in a
	False
	>>> 2 not in a
	False
		Returns True if element is present in tuple. Otherwise returns false.

Comparison	>>> a=(2,3,4,5,6,7,8,9,10)
	>>>b=(2,3,4)
	>>> a==b
	False
	>>> a!=b
	True
		Returns True if all elements in both elements are same. Otherwise returns false

Tuple is immutable so changes cannot be done on the elements of a tuple once it is assigned.

Methods	Example	Description

a.index(tuple)	>>> a=(1,2,3,4,5)
	>>> a.index(5)
	4
		Returns the index of the first matched item.

a.count(tuple)	>>>a=(1,2,3,4,5) >>> a.count(3) 1	Returns the count of the given element.
len(tuple)	>>> len(a) 5	Return the length of the tuple

min(tuple)	>>> min(a) 1	Return the minimum element in a tuple
max(tuple)	>>> max(a) 5	Return the maximum element in a tuple
del(tuple)	>>> del(a)	Delete the entire tuple.

4.2.5 Tuple Assignment

❖ Tuple assignment allows, variables on the left of an assignment operator and values of tuple on the right of the assignment operator.

❖ Multiple assignment works by creating a tuple of expressions from the right-hand side, and a tuple of targets from the left, and then matching each expression to a target.

❖ Because multiple assignments use tuples to work, it is often termed tuple assignment.

Uses of Tuple assignment:

It is often useful to swap the values of two variables.

Example:

Swapping using temporary variable	Swapping using tuple assignment
a=20 b=50 temp = a a = b b = temp print("value after swapping is",a,b)	a=20 b=50 (a,b)=(b,a) print("value after swapping is",a,b)

Multiple assignments:

Multiple values can be assigned to multiple variables using tuple assignment.

>>>(a,b,c)=(1,2,3)

>>>print(a)

1

>>>print(b)

2

>>>print(c)

3

4.2.6 Tuple as return value

- ❖ A Tuple is a comma separated sequence of items.
- ❖ It is created with or without ( ).
- ❖ A function can return one value. if you want to return more than one value from a function. we can use tuple as return value.

Example1:	Output:

`def div(a,b):`
`   r=a%b`
`   q=a//b`
`   return(r,q)`
`a=eval(input("enter a value:"))`
`b=eval(input("enter b value:"))`
`r,q=div(a,b)`
`print("reminder:",r)`
`print("quotient:",q)`
	enter a value:4
	enter b value:3
	reminder: 1
	quotient: 1

4.2.7 Tuple as Argument

The parameter name that begins with * gathers argument into a tuple.

Example	Output
def printall(*args): print(args) printall(2,3,'a')	(2, 3, 'a')

4.3 Dictionaries

❖ Dictionary is an unordered collection of elements. An element in dictionary has a key: value pair.

❖ All elements in dictionary are placed inside the curly braces i.e. { }

❖ Elements in Dictionaries are **accessed via keys** and not by their position.

❖ The values of a dictionary can be any data type.

❖ Keys must be immutable data type (numbers, strings, tuple)

4.3.1 <u>Operations on dictionary</u>

❖ Accessing an element
❖ Update
❖ Add element
❖ Membership

Operations	Example	Description

Creating a dictionary	>>> a={1:"one",2:"two"}
	>>> print(a)
	{1: 'one', 2: 'two'}
		Creating the dictionary with elements of different data types.

accessing an element	>>> a[1]
	'one'
	>>> a[0]
	KeyError: 0
		Accessing the elements by using keys.

Update	>>> a[1]="ONE"
	>>> print(a)
	{1: 'ONE', 2: 'two'}
		Assigning a new value to key. It replaces the old value by new value.

add element	>>> a[3]="three"
	>>> print(a)
	{1: 'ONE', 2: 'two', 3: 'three'}
		Add new element in to the dictionary with key.

membership	a={1: 'ONE', 2: 'two', 3: 'three'}
	>>> 1 in a
	True
	>>> 3 not in a
	False
		Returns True if the key is present in dictionary. Otherwise returns false.

4.3.2 Methods in Dictionary

Method	Example	Description

a.copy( )	a={1: 'ONE', 2: 'two', 3: 'three'}
	>>> b=a.copy()
	>>> print(b)
	{1: 'ONE', 2: 'two', 3: 'three'}
		It returns copy of the dictionary. here copy of dictionary 'a' get stored in to dictionary 'b'

a.items()	>>> a.items() dict_items([(1, 'ONE'), (2, 'two'), (3, 'three')])	Return a new view of the dictionary's items. It displays a list of dictionary's (key, value) tuple pairs.
a.keys()	>>> a.keys() dict_keys([1, 2, 3])	It displays list of keys in a dictionary
a.values()	>>> a.values() dict_values(['ONE', 'two', 'three'])	It displays list of values in dictionary

a.pop(key)	>>> a.pop(3)
	'three'
	>>> print(a)
	{1: 'ONE', 2: 'two'}
		Remove the element with *key* and return its value from the dictionary.

setdefault(key,value)	>>> a.setdefault(3,"three")
	'three'
	>>> print(a)
	{1: 'ONE', 2: 'two', 3: 'three'}
	>>> a.setdefault(2)
	'two'
		If key is in the dictionary, return its value. If key is not present, insert key with a value of dictionary and return dictionary.

a.update(dictionary)	>>> b={4:"four"}
	>>> a.update(b)
	>>> print(a)
	{1: 'ONE', 2: 'two', 3: 'three', 4: 'four'}
		It will add the dictionary with the existing dictionary

fromkeys()	>>> key={"apple","ball"}
	>>> value="for kids"
	>>> d=dict.fromkeys(key,value)
	>>> print(d)
	{'apple': 'for kids', 'ball': 'for kids'}
		It creates a dictionary from key and values.

len(a)	a={1: 'ONE', 2: 'two', 3: 'three'} >>>lena(a) 3	It returns the length of the list.
clear()	a={1: 'ONE', 2: 'two', 3: 'three'} >>>a.clear() >>>print(a) >>>{ }	Remove all elements form the dictionary.
del(a)	a={1: 'ONE', 2: 'two', 3: 'three'} >>> del(a)	It will delete the entire dictionary.

4.3.3 Difference Between List, Tuples and Dictionary

List	Tuples	Dictionary
A list is mutable	A tuple is immutable	A dictionary is mutable
Lists are dynamic	Tuples are fixed size in nature	In values can be of any data type and can repeat, keys must be of immutable type
List are enclosed in brackets[ ] and their elements and size can be changed	Tuples are enclosed in parenthesis ( ) and cannot be updated	Tuples are enclosed in curly braces { } and consist of key:value
Homogenous	Heterogeneous	Homogenous
Example: List = [10, 12, 15]	Example: Words = ("spam", "egss") Or Words = "spam", "eggs"	Example: Dict = {"ram": 26, "abi": 24}
Access: print(list[0])	Access: print(words[0])	Access: print(dict["ram"])
Can contain duplicate elements	Can contain duplicate elements. Faster compared to lists	Cant contain duplicate keys, but can contain duplicate values
Slicing can be done	Slicing can be done	Slicing can't be done
Usage: ❖ List is used if a collection of data that doesnt need random access. ❖ List is used when data can be modified frequently	Usage: ❖ Tuple can be used when data cannot be changed. ❖ A tuple is used in combination with a dictionary i.e.a tuple might represent a key.	Usage: ❖ Dictionary is used when a logical association between key:value pair. ❖ When in need of fast lookup for data, based on a custom key. ❖ Dictionary is used when data is being constantly modified.

4.4 Advanced List Processing

4.4.1 List Comprehension

❖ List comprehensions provide a concise way to apply operations on a list.

❖ It creates a new list in which each element is the result of applying a given operation in a list.

❖ It consists of brackets containing an expression followed by a "for" clause, then a list.

❖ The list comprehension always returns a result list.

Syntax

list=[expression for item in list if conditional]

List Comprehension	Output
>>>L=[x**2 for x in range(0,5)] >>>print(L)	[0, 1, 4, 9, 16]
>>>[x for x in range(1,10) if x%2==0]	[2, 4, 6, 8]
>>>[x for x in 'Python Programming' if x in ['a','e','i','o','u']]	['o', 'o', 'a', 'i']
>>>mixed=[1,2,"a",3,4.2] >>> [x**2 for x in mixed if type(x)==int]	[1, 4, 9]
>>>[x+3 for x in [1,2,3]]	[4, 5, 6]
>>> [x*x for x in range(5)]	[0, 1, 4, 9, 16]
>>> num=[-1,2,-3,4,-5,6,-7] >>> [x for x in num if x>=0]	[2, 4, 6]

>>> str=["this","is","an","example"]
>>> element=[word[0] for word in str]
>>> print(element)
	['t', 'i', 'a', 'e']

4.4.2 Nested List

List inside another list is called nested list.

```
Python 3.7.6 Shell                                    —    □    ×
File  Edit  Shell  Debug  Options  Window  Help
>>> m=[23,6,32,[12,14]]
>>> m[1]
6
>>> m[3]
[12, 14]
>>> m[3][1]
14
>>> |
                                              Ln: 258  Col: 4
```

Matrix Addition Program

```python
a=[[1,1],[1,1]]
b=[[2,2],[2,2]]
c=[[0,0],[0,0]]
for i in range(len(a)):
    for j in range(len(b)):
        c[i][j]=a[i][j]+b[i][j]
print("Matrix Addition is:")
for i in c:
    print(i)
```

```
>>>
= RESTART: C:/Program Files/PYTHON/matadd.py
Matrix Addition is:
[3, 3]
[3, 3]
>>>
```

ILLUSTRATIVE PROBLEMS

SELECTION SORT

```python
def selection(a):
    for i in range(0,len(a)):
        for j in range(i+1,len(a)):
            if(a[j]<a[i]):
                temp=a[i]
                a[i]=a[j]
                a[j]=temp
a=[2,1,4,6,3]
print("======SELECTION SORT======")
print("list of elements before sorting :",a)
selection(a)
print("list of elements after sorting:",a)
```

```
Python 3.7.6 Shell                                    —    □    ×
File  Edit  Shell  Debug  Options  Window  Help
>>>
=== RESTART: C:\Program Files\PYTHON\SS.py ==
=====SELECTION SORT======
list of elements before sorting : [2, 1, 4, 6, 3]
list of elements after sorting: [1, 2, 3, 4, 6]
>>>
                                                      Ln: 268  Col: 4
```

INSERTION SORT

```
IS.py - C:\Program Files\PYTHON\IS.py (3.7.6)           —    □    ×
File  Edit  Format  Run  Options  Window  Help
print("=========INSERTION SORT==========
a=[3,2,4,1,5]
print("List of elements before sorting:",a)
for i in a:
    j=a.index(i)
    while j>0:
        if(a[j-1]>a[j]):
            temp=a[j-1]
            a[j-1]=a[j]
            a[j]=temp
        else:
            break
        j=j-1
print ("list of elements after sorting:",a)
                                          Ln: 1  Col: 0
```

```
Python 3.7.6 Shell                          —    □    X
File  Edit  Shell  Debug  Options  Window  Help
>>>

===== RESTART: C:\Program Files\PYTHON\IS.py =====
==========INSERTION SORT============
list of elements before sorting: [3, 2, 4, 1, 5]
list of elements after sorting: [1, 2, 3, 4, 5]
>>>
                                          Ln: 273  Col: 4
```

MERGE SORT

```
MS.py - C:\Program Files\PYTHON\MS.py (3.7.6)                    —    □    ×
File  Edit  Format  Run  Options  Window  Help
def mergesort(alist):
    print("splitting",alist)
    if(len(alist)>1):
        mid=len(alist)//2
        lefthalf=alist[:mid]
        righthalf=alist[mid:]
        mergesort(lefthalf)
        mergesort(righthalf)
        i=0
        j=0
        k=0
        while(i<len(lefthalf) and j<len(righthalf)):
            if(lefthalf[i]<righthalf[j]):
                alist[k]=lefthalf[i]
                i=i+1
            else:
                alist[k]=righthalf[j]
                j=j+1
            k=k+1
        while(i<len(lefthalf)):
            alist[k]=leftthalf[i]
            i=i+1
            k=k+1
        while(j<len(righthalf)):
            alist[k]=righthalf[j]
            j=j+1
            k=k+1
print("=========MERGE SORT==============")
alist=[54,26,93,17,77,897,8765]
print("merging",alist)
mergesort(alist)
print(alist)
                                                                Ln: 1  Col: 0
```

```
Python 3.7.6 Shell                                                    —    □    ×
File  Edit  Shell  Debug  Options  Window  Help
>>>
============== RESTART: C:\Program Files\PYTHON\MS.py =============
=============MERGE SORT===============
merging [54, 26, 93, 17, 77, 897, 8765]
splitting [54, 26, 93, 17, 77, 897, 8765]
splitting [54, 26, 93]
splitting [54]
splitting [26, 93]
splitting [26]
splitting [93]
splitting [17, 77, 897, 8765]
splitting [17, 77]
splitting [17]
splitting [77]
splitting [897, 8765]
splitting [897]
splitting [8765]
[17, 26, 54, 77, 93, 897, 8765]
                                                              Ln: 291  Col: 4
```

QUICK SORT

```
QS.py - C:/Program Files/PYTHON/QS.py (3.7.6)          —    □    ×
File  Edit  Format  Run  Options  Window  Help
def partition(arr,low,high):
    i = ( low-1 )
    pivot = arr[high]
    for j in range(low , high):
        if arr[j] <= pivot:
            i = i+1
            arr[i],arr[j] = arr[j],arr[i]
    arr[i+1],arr[high] = arr[high],arr[i+1]
    return ( i+1 )
def quickSort(arr,low,high):
    if low < high:
        pi = partition(arr,low,high)
        quickSort(arr, low, pi-1)
        quickSort(arr, pi+1, high)
arr = [2,5,3,8,6,5,4,7]
n = len(arr)
quickSort(arr,0,n-1)
print("=========QUICK SORT=========")
print ("Sorted array is:")
for i in range(n):
    print (arr[i],end=" ")
                                                      Ln: 21  Col: 26
```

```
Python 3.7.6 Shell                                                    —    □    ×
File  Edit  Shell  Debug  Options  Window  Help
Python 3.7.6 (tags/v3.7.6:43364a7ae0, Dec 19 2019, 00:42:30) [MSC v.1916 64 bit
(AMD64)] on win32
Type "help", "copyright", "credits" or "license()" for more information.
>>>
==================== RESTART: C:\Program Files\PYTHON\QS.py ====================
========QUICK SORT========
Sorted array is:
2 3 4 5 5 6 7 8
>>>
                                                                      Ln: 8  Col: 4
```

CHAPTER 5

FILES, MODULES AND PACKAGES

> **Files**: text files, reading and writing files, format operator, command line arguments, **Errors and Exceptions**: handling exceptions, **Modules, Packages**; Illustrative programs: word count, copy file.

5.1 FILES

❖ File is a named location on disk to store related information. It is used to permanently store data in a memory (e.g. hard disk).

5.1.1 File Types

❖ Text file
❖ Binary file

Text File	Binary file
Text file is a sequence of characters that can be sequentially processed by a computer in forward direction.	A binary files store the data in the binary format (i.e. 0's and 1's)
Each line is terminated with a special character, called the EOL or End of Line character	It contains any type of data (PDF, images, Word doc, Spreadsheet, Zip files,etc)

5.1.2 Operations on Files

In Python, a file operation takes place in the following order,

❖ Opening a file

❖ Reading / Writing file

❖ Closing the file

How to open a file:

Syntax	Example
file_object=open("file_name.txt","mode")	f=open("sample.txt","w")

How to create a file:

Syntax	Example
file_object=open("file_name.txt","mode") file_object.write(string) file_object.close()	f=open("sample.txt","w") f.write("hello") f.close()
Modes	**Description**
r	read only mode
w	write only
a	appending mode
r+	read and write mode
w+	write and read mode

5.1.3 Modes in file

Differentiate write and append mode:

Write Mode	Append Mode
It is use to write a string into a file.	It is used to append (add) a string into a file.
If file does not exist it creates a new file.	If file does not exist it creates a new file.
If file exists in the specified name, the existing content will overwrite in a file by the given string.	It will add the string at the end of the old file.

5.1.4 File Operation and Methods

S.No	Syntax	Example	Description
1	f.write(string)	f.write("hello")	Writing a string into a file.
2	f.writelines(sequence)	f.writelines("1st line \n second line")	Writes a sequence of strings to the file.
3	f.read(size)	f.read( ) #read entire file f.read(4) #read the first 4 charecter	To read the content of a file.
4	f.readline( )	f.readline( )	Reads one line at a time.
5	f.readlines( )	f.readlines( )	Reads the entire file and returns a list of lines.
6	f.seek(offset,whence) whence value is optional.	f.seek(0)	Move the file pointer to the appropriate position. It sets the file pointer to the starting of the file.
	whence =0 from begining	f.seek(3,0)	Move three character from the beginning.
	whence =1 from current position	f.seek(3,1)	Move three character ahead from the current position.
	whence =2 from last position	f.seek(-1,2)	Move to the first character from end of the file
7	f.tell( )	f.tell( )	Get the current file pointer position.
8	f.flush( )	f.flush( )	To flush the data before closing any file.
9	f.close( )	f.close( )	Close an open file.
10	f.name	f.name o/p: 1.txt	Return the name of the file.
11	f.mode	f.mode o/p: w	Return the Mode of file.
12	os.rename(old name,new name)	import os os.rename("1.txt","2.txt")	Renames the file or directory.
13	os.remove(file name)	import os os.remove("2.txt")	Remove the file.

5.1.5 Format Operator

The argument of write( ) has to be a string, so if we want to put other values along with the string in a file, we have to convert them to strings.

Convert no into string:	output

>>> x = 52
 	
>>> f.write(str(x))
	"52"

Convert to strings using format operator, %	**Example:**
print ("format string"%(tuple of values)) file.write("format string"%(tuple of values)	>>>age=13 >>>print("The age is %d"%age) The age is 13
Program to write even number in a file using format operator	**OutPut**

f=open("t.txt","w")
n=eval(input("enter n:"))
for i in range(n):
    a=int(input("enter number:"))
    if(a%2==0):
f.write(a)
f.close()
	enter n:4
	enter number:3
	enter number:4
	enter number:6
	enter number:8
	result in file t.txt 4
	6
	8

- ❖ The first operand is the format string, which specifies how the second operand is formatted.
- ❖ The result is a string. For example, the format sequence '%d' means that the second operand should be formatted as an integer (d stands for "decimal"):

Format character	Description
%c	Character
%s	String formatting
%d	Decimal integer
%f	Floating point real number

5.1.6 Command Line Argument

- ❖ The command line argument is used to pass input from the command line to your program when they are started to execute.
- ❖ Handling command line arguments with Python need sys module.
- ❖ sys module provides information about constants, functions and methods of the pyhton interpretor.

argv[ ] is used to access the command line argument. The argument list starts from 0. sys.argv[0]= gives file name

sys.argv[1]=provides access to the first input

Example 1 cmd.py
import sys print("the file name is %s" %(sys.argv[0]))
addition of two num (cmd1.py)
import sys a= sys.argv[1] b= sys.argv[2] sum=int(a)+int(b) print("Sum is:",sum)
Word count using comment line arg: (cmd2.py)

from sys import argv
a = argv[1].split()
dict = {}
for i in a:
    if i in dict:
        dict[i]=dict[i]+1
    else:
dict[i] = 1
print(dict)
print(len(a))

```
Administrator: Command Prompt                                          —    □    ×

C:\Program Files\PYTHON>python cmd.py
the file name is cmd.py

C:\Program Files\PYTHON>python cmd1.py 56 67
Sum is: 123

C:\Program Files\PYTHON>

C:\Program Files\PYTHON>python cmd2.py "Welcome to python program lets code in python"
{'Welcome': 1, 'to': 1, 'python': 2, 'program': 1, 'lets': 1, 'code': 1, 'in': 1}
Length of the String is: 8

C:\Program Files\PYTHON>
```

5.2 Errors and Exception

5.2.1 Errors

Errors are the mistakes in the program also referred as bugs. They are almost always the fault of the programmer. The process of finding and eliminating errors is called debugging. Errors can be classified into three major groups:

- ❖ Syntax errors
- ❖ Runtime errors
- ❖ Logical errors

5.2.1.1 Syntax errors

- ❖ Syntax errors are the errors which are displayed when the programmer do mistakes when writing a program.
- ❖ When a program has syntax errors it will not get executed.
- ❖ Common Python syntax errors include:

  - Leaving out a keyword
  - Putting a keyword in the wrong place
  - Leaving out a symbol, such as a colon, comma or brackets
  - Misspelling a keyword
  - Incorrect indentation
  - Empty block

5.2.1.2 *Runtime errors*

❖ If a program is syntactically correct – that is, free of syntax errors – it will be run by the Python interpreter.

❖ However, the program may exit unexpectedly during execution if it encounters a runtime error.

❖ When a program has runtime error, I will get executed but it will not produce output.

❖ Common Python runtime errors include:

- Division by zero
- Performing an operation on incompatible types
- Using an identifier which has not been defined
- Accessing a list element, dictionary value or object attribute which doesn't exist
- Trying to access a file which doesn't exist

5.2.1.3 *Logical errors*

❖ Logical errors are the most difficult to fix.

❖ They occur when the program runs without crashing, but produces an incorrect result.

❖ Common Python logical errors include:

- Using the wrong variable name
- Indenting a block to the wrong level
- Using integer division instead of floating-point division
- Getting operator precedence wrong
- Making a mistake in a boolean expression

5.2.2 **Exceptions**

❖ An exception (runtime time error) is an error, which occurs during the execution of a program that disrupts the normal flow of the program's instructions.

❖ When a Python script raises an exception, it must either handle the exception immediately otherwise it terminates or quit.

S.No.	Exception Name	Description
1	FloatingPointError	Raised when a floating-point calculation fails.
2	ZeroDivisionError	Raised when division or modulo by zero takes place for all numeric types.
3	AttributeError	Raised in case of failure of attribute reference or assignment.
4	ImportError	Raised when an import statement fails.
5	KeyboardInterrupt	Raised when the user interrupts program execution, usually by pressing Ctrl+c.
6	IndexError	Raised when an index is not found in a sequence
7	KeyError	Raised when the specified key is not found in the dictionary.
8	NameError	Raised when an identifier is not found in the local or global name space
9	IOError	Raised when an input/ output operation fails, such as the print statement or the open() function when trying to open a file that does not exist.
10	SyntaxError	Raised when there is an error in Python syntax.
11	IndentationError	Raised when indentation is not specified properly.
12	SystemError	Raised when the interpreter finds an internal problem, but when this error is encountered the Python interpreter does not exit.

13	SystemExit	Raised when Python interpreter is quit by using the sys.exit() function. If not handled in the code, causes the interpreter to exit.
14	TypeError	Raised when an operation or function is attempted that is invalid for the specified data type.
15	ValueError	Raised when the built-in function for a data type has the valid type of arguments, but the arguments have invalid values specified.
16	RuntimeError	Raised when a generated error does not fall into any category.

5.2.3 Exception Handling

❖ Exception handling is done by try and catch block.

❖ Suspicious code that may raise an exception, this kind of code will be placed in try block.

❖ A block of code which handles the problem is placed in except block.

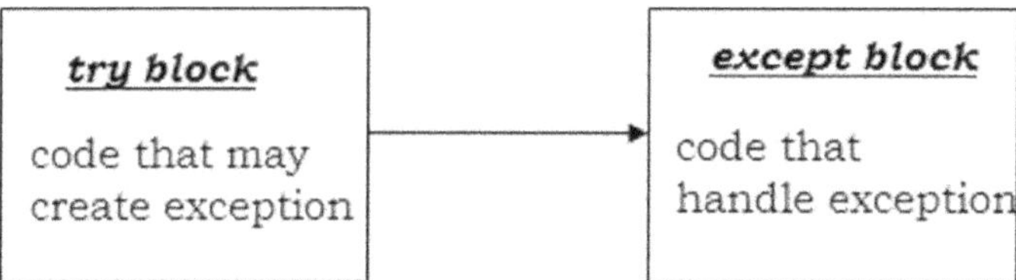

Catching Exceptions:

1. try...except
2. try...except...inbuilt exception
3. try... except...else
4. try...except...else....finally
5. try.. except..except..
6. try...raise..except..

try ... except

- ❖ In Python, exceptions can be handled using a try statement.
- ❖ A critical operation which can raise exception is placed inside the try clause and the code that handles exception is written in except clause.
- ❖ It is up to us, what operations we perform once we have caught the exception. Here is a simple example.

Syntax

try:

code that create exception

except:

exception handling statement

Example	Output

try:
    age=int(input("enter age:"))
    print("Age is:",age)
except:
    print("enter a valid age")
	enter age:8
	Age is: 8
	enter age:f
	enter a valid age

try...except...inbuilt exception

Syntax

try:

code that create exception

except inbuilt exception:

exception handling statement

Example	Output

try:
    age=int(input("enter age:"))
    print("Age is:",age)
except ValueError:
    print("enter a valid age")
	enter age:d
	
	enter a valid age

try ... except ... else clause

- ❖ Else part will be executed only if the try block doesn't raise an exception.
- ❖ Python will try to process all the statements inside try block. If value error occurs, the flow of control will immediately pass to the except block and remaining statement in try block will be skipped.

Syntax

try:

*   code that create exception*

except:

*   exception handling statement*

else:

statements

Example program	Output

try:
    age=int(input("enter your age:"))
except ValueError:
print("entered value is not a number")
else:
    print("Age is:",age)
	enter your age: six
	entered value is not a number
	enter your age:6
	Age is: 6

try ... except...finally

A finally clause is always executed before leaving the try statement, whether an exception has occurred or not.

Syntax

try:

   code that create exception

except:

   exception handling statement

else:

   statements

finally:

statements

Example program	Output

try:
   age=int(input("enter your age:"))
except ValueError:
   print("entered value is not a number")
else:
   print("Age is:",age)
finally:
print("Thank you")
	enter your age: six
	entered value is not a number
	Thank you
	enter your age:5
	Age is 5
	Thank you

try...multiple exception:

Syntax

try:

code that create exception

except:

exception handling statement

except:

statements

Example	Output:
a=int(input("enter a:"))	enter a:2
b=int(input("enter b:"))	enter b:0
try:	Cannot divide by zero
c=a/b	enter a:2
print(c)	enter b: h
except ZeroDivisionError:	It is not a number
print("Cannot divide by zero")	
except ValueError:	
print("It is not a number")	

Raising Exceptions

In Python programming, exceptions are raised when corresponding errors occur at run time, but we can forcefully raise it using the keyword raise.

Syntax:

>>> raise error name

Example:	Output:

``
try:
    age=int(input("enter your age:"))
    if (age<0):
        raise ValueError("Age can't be negative")
except ValueError:
        print("you have entered incorrect age")
else:
print("your age is:",age)
``
	enter your age:-7
	
	Age can't be negative

5.3 MODULES

- ❖ A module is a file containing Python definitions, functions, statements and instructions.
- ❖ Standard library of Python is extended as modules.
- ❖ To use modules in a program, programmer needs to import the module.
- ❖ To get information about the functions and variables supported module you can use the built-in function help (Module name), Eg: help("math").
- ❖ The dir() function is used to list the variables and functions defined inside a module. If an argument, i.e., a module name is passed to the dir, it returns that modules variables and function names else it returns the details of the current module. Eg: dir(math)

OS module

- ❖ The OS module in python provides functions for interacting with the operating system
- ❖ To access the OS module have to import the OS module in our program

import os

```
Python 3.7.6 Shell                                    —   □   ✕
File  Edit  Shell  Debug  Options  Window  Help
00:42:30) [MSC v.1916 64 bit (AMD64)] on win32
Type "help", "copyright", "credits" or "license()"
for more information.
>>> import os
>>> print(os.name)
nt
>>> print(os.getcwd())
C:\Program Files\PYTHON
>>>
                                              Ln: 8  Col: 4
```

mkdir(folder)	os.mkdir("python")	Create a directory(folder) with the given name.
rename(oldname, new name)	os.rename("python","pspp")	Rename the directory or folder
remove("folder")	os.remove("pspp")	Remove (delete) the directory or folder.
getuid( )	os.getuid( )	Return the current process's user id.
environ	os.environ	Get the users environment

Sys module

- ❖ Sys module provides information about constants, functions and methods.
- ❖ It provides access to some variables used or maintained by the interpreter.

import sys

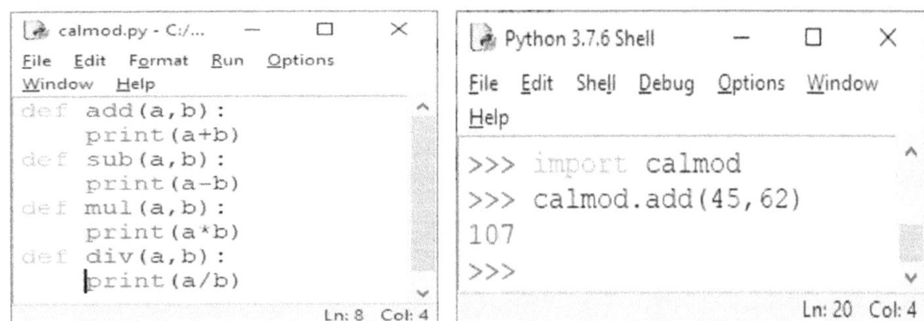

```
Python 3.7.6 Shell                                             –   □   ×
File  Edit  Shell  Debug  Options  Window  Help
>>> import sys
>>> print(sys.path)
['', 'C:\\Program Files\\PYTHON\\Lib\\idlelib', 'C:\\Program Files\\PYTHON\\py
thon37.zip', 'C:\\Program Files\\PYTHON\\DLLs', 'C:\\Program Files\\PYTHON\\li
b', 'C:\\Program Files\\PYTHON', 'C:\\Users\\Deepak\\AppData\\Roaming\\Python\
\Python37\\site-packages', 'C:\\Program Files\\PYTHON\\lib\\site-packages', 'C
:\\Program Files\\PYTHON\\lib\\site-packages\\win32', 'C:\\Program Files\\PYTH
ON\\lib\\site-packages\\win32\\lib', 'C:\\Program Files\\PYTHON\\lib\\site-pac
kages\\Pythonwin']
>>> print(sys.platform)
win32
>>> print(sys.argv)
['']
>>> sys.exit
<built-in function exit>
                                                              Ln: 17  Col: 4
```

Steps to create the own module

Here we are going to create calc module: our modules contains four functions (i.e) add(),sub(),mul(),div()

```
calmod.py - C:/...        –   □   ×
File  Edit  Format  Run  Options
Window  Help
def  add(a,b):
     print(a+b)
def  sub(a,b):
     print(a-b)
def  mul(a,b):
     print(a*b)
def  div(a,b):
     print(a/b)
                          Ln: 8  Col: 4
```

```
Python 3.7.6 Shell        –   □   ×
File  Edit  Shell  Debug  Options  Window
Help
>>> import calmod
>>> calmod.add(45,62)
107
>>>
                          Ln: 20  Col: 4
```

5.4 PACKAGE:

- ❖ A package is a collection of Python modules. Module is a single Python file containing function definitions; a package is a directory (folder) of Python modules containing an additional _init_.py file, to differentiate a package from a directory.
- ❖ Packages can be nested to any depth, provided that the corresponding directories contain their own _init_.py file.

❖ _init_.py file is a directory indicates to the python interpreter that the directory should be treated like a python package. _init_.py is used to initialize the python package.

Steps to create a package

Step 1: Create the Package Directory

Create a directory(folder) and give it your package's name. Here the package name is calculator.

	This PC › Windows (C:) › Program Files › PYTHON			
	Name	Date modified	Type	Size
Quick access				
	pycache	08-05-2021 15:16	File folder	
OneDrive	CALC_PACK	08-05-2021 15:25	File folder	
This PC	DLLs	15-12-2020 11:50	File folder	

Step 2: write Modules for CALC_PACK directory add save the modules in calculator directory.

Here four modules have created for calculator directory.

	This PC › Windows (C:) › Program Files › PYTHON › CALC_PACK			
	Name	Date modified	Type	Size
	adddemo	08-05-2021 15:27	Python File	1 KB
	difdemo	08-05-2021 15:27	Python File	1 KB
	divdemo	08-05-2021 15:28	Python File	1 KB
	proddemo	08-05-2021 15:28	Python File	1 KB

adddemo.py	difdemo.py	proddemo.py	divdemo.py
def add(a,b):	def dif(a,b):	def prod(a,b):	def div(a,b):
print(a+b)	print(a-b)	print(a*b)	print(a/b)

Step 3: Add the _init_.py File in the calculator directory

A directory must contain a file named _init_.py in order for Python to consider it as a package.

Add the following code in the _init_.py file

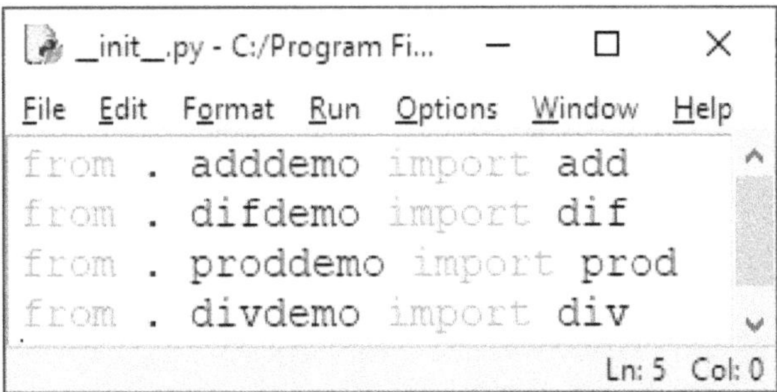

Step 4:To test your package.

Import CALC_PACK package in your program and add the path of your package in your program by using sys.path.append().

Here the path is "C:\Program Files\PYTHON"

```
import CALC_PACK
import sys
sys.path.append("C:\Program Files\PYTHON")
print(CALC_PACK.add(23,45))
print(CALC_PACK.dif(67,34))
print(CALC_PACK.prod(42,12))
print(CALC_PACK.div(36,18))
```

```
=========================================== RESTART: C:/Program Files/PYTHON/packagedemo.py ====
68

33

504

2.0
```

ILLUSTRATIVE PROGRAMS

WORD COUNT OF A FILE

```
print("=========WORD COUNT FROM A FILE===========")
fname=input("Enter a file name:")
num_words=0
with open(fname,'r') as f:
    for line in f:
        words=line.split()
num_words=num_words+len(words)
print("number of words:",num_words)
```

```
>>>
=========================================== RESTART: C:\Program Fil
es\PYTHON\word_count.py ===========================================
=========WORD COUNT FROM A FILE===========
Enter a file name:Output.txt
number of words: 9
>>>
```

FILE COPY

```
#to create a copy of a file
print("=========COPY A FILE===========")
f1=open("Input.txt","r")
f2=open("OutputFile.txt","w")
for i in f1:
    f2.write(i)
f1.close()
f2.close()
```

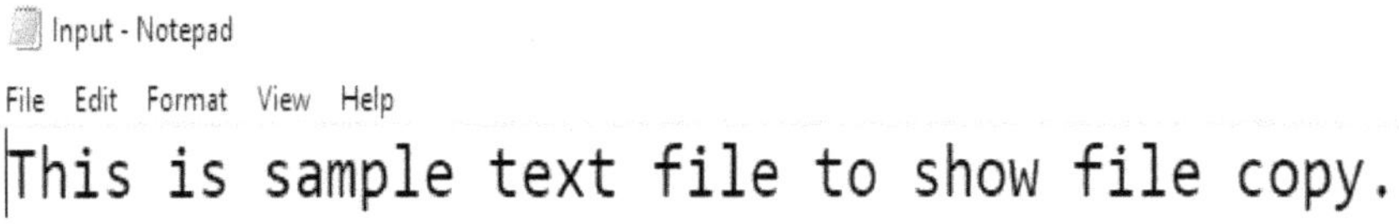

Input - Notepad

File   Edit   Format   View   Help

This is sample text file to show file copy.

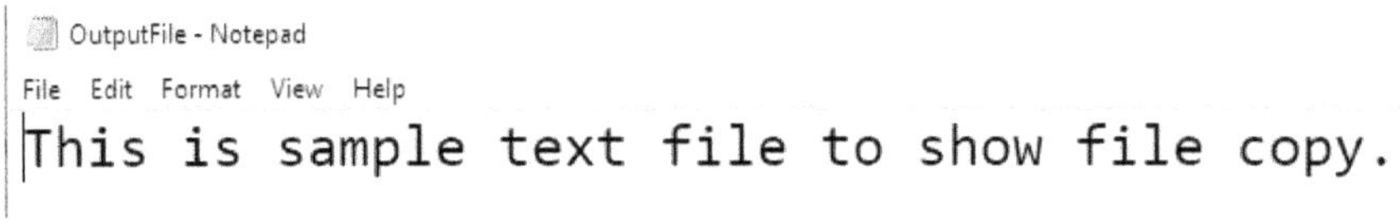

OutputFile - Notepad

File   Edit   Format   View   Help

This is sample text file to show file copy.